Wanting More

Growing in God and Service to the World

Wanting More

Growing in God and Service to the World

By Joel Vestal

Foreword by Louie Giglio

ServLife International, Inc.

"Joel Vestal listens and learns, as evidenced in *Wanting More*. Through this autobiographical journal of a remarkable pilgrimage, the reader gains insight into the holistic nature of the mission of God and the power that is available to those committed to faithfully serve that mission."

Dr. Bill O'Brien, Founder & Former Director
The Global Center of Beeson Divinity School; Samford University
Birmingham, AL

"I have known Joel Vestal since he was a senior in high school. In 28 years of ministry, I have never known someone who is more passionate, gifted, and anointed in the area of telling the story of Jesus. The collection of stories which represent Joel's experiences as he has traveled are guaranteed to refresh the spirit of the reader and perhaps even challenge to attempt greater things for God. This is a wonderful book which is part biography, part devotional, and part 'how to' in missions. My only regret is that it is only a small portion of all of the stories that Joel has to share—and that others have to share about Joel and his passion to take Jesus to the nations."

Dr. R. Allen Jackson, Associate Professor of Youth Education
New Orleans Baptist Theological Seminary
New Orleans, LA

"It has been said that preaching is not so much the preparation and delivery of a sermon, as it is the preparation and presentation of a *person.* Likewise, Joel Vestal's book is not so much the preparation and publication of a manuscript as it is the preparation and sharing of a *soul.* Jesus Christ is glorified in this inspiring book because *Jesus Christ is glorified in Joel Vestal's life and ministry.* When Joel Vestal speaks, I listen; when Joel Vestal writes, I read. To God be the glory!"

Dr. Randall O'Brien, Professor and Chair
Department of Religion: Baylor University; Waco, TX

CONTENTS

ACKNOWLEDGEMENTS

First, I wish to thank my wife, Jill Elise. Your love, support, companionship, and encouragement mean more than you know. I love you. To my son, Zayd, who has been my little inspiration as we have dragged him to the Himalayas, the beaches of Thailand, the tallest building in the world in Kuala Lumpur, and the villages in India—all before he turned one. You will be the envy of all your future classmates when it is "Show & Tell" day!

To Sivin Kit in Kuala Lumpur and his help in the printing of this book; Albert and Pushpa Das and family in India; all the ServLife India church planters and staff; all the children at our children's homes; my friends and co-laborers in Kathmandu, Nepal, Isu Karki, Ram P. Shrestha, Udaya and Bhakti Bhatta; Joseph Hakim Oloya in Sudan; James and Julia Smith in Houston; Heather Green in Atlanta; Michael Warden, my editor in Austin; Mo Andrieu in Las Vegas; Jennifer Ball in Colorado; the love and support of my father and mother, Daniel and Earlene Vestal; all the individuals, foundations, churches, organizations, and companies that support ServLife's work around the world; other ServLife board members throughout the years, Ron Gabriel, Clint Green, Laura Kennemer, David Fielder, Catherine King, Jerry Wilkinson, Steve Rhodes, Charlie Dodd, Ty Denney, Larry Morris, Mike Thomas, Tim Russell, Chris Bryan and Ross Purdy—my deepest gratitude to you all.

And, ultimately, my thanks belongs to the One who is the giver of all good things—the Lord Jesus Christ.

FOREWORD

By Louie Giglio

A few things were crystal clear to me the very first time I met Joel Vestal. For one, I knew right away that he cared deeply about the people of the world and was burdened about the injustice, poverty and spiritual darkness that were a way of life for so many. I also knew in that first encounter that Joel wasn't waiting for permission from anybody to do something to help them, especially given the fact that Jesus had already entrusted to him the mission of communicating to them in tangible ways His love and kindness.

Joel was only a college freshman. But he was a man with a purpose that encompassed the nations.

While a lot of other students were innocently immersed in conversations about their social lives (or lack thereof) or some other hot cultural topic, Joel was talking about unreached people groups and ways to connect them to God's redemption story. And he wasn't just reciting statistics and spouting off information, his heart was pulsing with compassion and an urgency to act—*now*. Before long, Joel had forged an alliance with a pastor in a remote region of India where few others dared to go and where the Gospel was seldom, if ever, heard.

To be completely honest, at first glance I thought Joel was a little over-zealous and had a lot to learn. But over time my reservation morphed into admiration and respect as the little seed he had planted in Bihar, India sprouted to become ServLife International, the fruit of one solitary student emboldened by the Spirit of God and determined to leverage his life so that people all over the world could hear the name of Jesus Christ.

It's staggering to think just how many people on the planet have never heard of Jesus—much less any of His life-giving words. Like us, they wonder about the meaning of life and are longing for their Maker. Yet they have never heard of Jesus Christ—the unique Son of God come to earth, the Divine in human flesh, the Father's gracious sacrifice for all our sins.

And we're not just talking about a handful of people in some remote village deep in the Amazon jungle, but countless millions—hundreds of millions—without Christ, dotting every continent on earth. Most are clustered in central Asia where China and India alone are home to over 2.3 billion people. That's why it's no surprise that right smack in the middle of that region, in a town in northern India near the Nepalese border, Joel first raised the ServLife banner, announcing the Kingdom of God.

Yet, equally staggering is the number of us who *have* heard of Jesus Christ—and call him Savior—that have failed to take seriously His last words to us. Recorded at the close of Matthew and Mark's Gospel accounts and in the first chapter of the book of Acts, those words propel us outward with a clear mission mandate to take His story to every person on earth.

I don't think Jesus was implying that we all should be "missionaries" in the traditional western sense of that word; rather, that we should lead "mission lifestyles," being concerned about the well being of all people and creatively using our gifts and means to bring them hope now and the message of life that never ends.

While people in every generation have eagerly and sacrificially answered that call, I'm encouraged to see a new wave of young people emerge with a passion to amplify God's fame among the nations at all cost. I think you'll be inspired (and convicted) to join them after reading Joel's book. And not out of a sense of guilt, but as the natural overflow of what He has so generously lavished on us.

As you go, Joel and his wife Elise will be right there with you, blazing a trail with their words and actions, compelling countless others to follow; me included.

At the end of the day, this God-mission to preach good news and bring restoration to every man, woman and child alive will succeed, ushering in the end of life as we know it and the coming of Christ. I want to be standing (kneeling) in that moment knowing that my life's influence extended past the edge of the subdivision and beyond the halls of the office. I want to be able to eternally rejoice, knowing that God allowed me to play a role in gathering every tribe and tongue to proclaim His praise. I think in that moment, everything else in life will pale in comparison to that reward.

Louie Giglio, Founder
Passion Conferences
www.passionnow.org

INTRODUCTION

Our lives are like a web of many connecting parts. Just as there are many parts in a car engine or a human body, which all must be active and connected to make the whole entity work, so are we as individuals in our relationship with God. Often the church has separated out the different parts of our Christian faith and made us think that our prayers and devotional life have nothing to do with how we choose to live in community with the world. How does our worship of God impact our understanding of persecution and suffering? How is our personal relationship with Him directly connected to the ways we choose to demonstrate love to our neighbors—including those neighbors who live halfway around the globe?

Augustine wrote that the older we grow in faith the less we like to be instructed—but we all need to be reminded. This book will take you on a journey across the globe and at the same time remind you of some important keys for your own spiritual journey here at home. Perhaps it will bring instruction for some as well. My hope is that it will leave you wanting more. You don't have to buy a plane ticket or get your passport to travel on this journey with me (though perhaps you will want to after reading this book!). It is a sad reality that only 15 percent of Americans even own a passport. But I wish to take you to far off corners of the world and share with you different experiences and encounters that have truly shaped me and allowed me to understand and know more of God and the world we live in.

I wish to share with you how God is transforming me, and I pray that through reading this book, you will allow God to transform you as well. I have a long way to go and many things that need to be worked on in my own journey. This book is part autobiography, part spiritual formation manual, and part mission book. But it is all written out of love and a desire to see God's kingdom expanded around the world.

I am in debt to countless people, both living and dead, who have helped mold me and who have taught me what it means to follow Jesus Christ. The ideas that are expressed in this book have come through many conversations, encounters with people throughout the world whom God has blessed me to meet, books, and listening to others share their stories and experiences.

If there are two admonitions I have for any reader of this book, young or old, they are these: First, that you will seize the opportunity to travel and see your life, faith and the Kingdom of God from a different ethnic, economic and, perhaps, a political perspective other than your own. There is an African proverb that says, "He who does not travel thinks his mother is the best cook. But the one who travels knows his mother is among other good cooks." The diversity of thoughts, colors, tastes, rituals and cultures in the world could only have been created by the greatest artist of all time, our Creator. I believe if we do not build global community, heaven is going to be a shock for many of us. I encourage you to seek out global community for yourself, your family and your local church. You will gain new and fresh perspectives of God you may not have seen before.

My second admonition, which is even greater than the first, is that your hunger for God will awaken and grow beyond your wildest imagination. I hope you will want more of God. You will want to know Him, to hunger for Him, and to glorify Him. There are many views on where to find God. As Christians, we first look to Jesus Christ, the living Word, and to Scripture, where we come to know God; however, I believe there are many places you can meet God where you may be least likely to look. Perhaps that place is in an art gallery, watching a film, looking at an old photograph, being among the poor, exploring nature, experiencing the death of someone close to you, getting married, becoming a parent, or building a close relationship.

People spend their whole lives seeking, searching and wanting to connect with their Maker. You cannot grow in this pursuit unless you hunger for it. You cannot hunger for it unless your appetite is aroused. Through this book, I pray your appetite is aroused to pursue a loving God with all of your mind, soul and strength, and that you come to love your neighbor as yourself. In the words of Jim Elliott, "Don't give yourselves to what others can do but will not do, but give yourselves to what others cannot do and will not do!"

Wanting More!
Joel Vestal

CHAPTER
1

The Bride is Bigger than You Think

"Kingdom people seek first the Kingdom of God and its justice; church people often put church work above concerns of justice, mercy and truth. Church people think about how to get people into the church; Kingdom people think about how to get the church into the world. Church people worry that the world might change the church; Kingdom people work to see the church change the world."—Howard Snyder

"Just as one could not speak of the church without speaking of its mission, it was impossible to think of the church without thinking, in the same breath, of the world to which it is sent."
—David Bosch

"The church is both the goal and the agent of world evangelization. Mission disengagement from the church is a biblical oxymoron."—Frank Severn

We left the capital of Kampala, Uganda on a small plane to visit the refugees from Sudan who fled the civil war raging in their homeland for decades. Since this was my first time to go the Sudan region, I was on the edge of my seat with anticipation. I could not imagine a region where war had ravaged a country for decades—killing millions and displacing millions more, making them refugees and internally-displaced civilians.

Once on the plane, I quickly realized I was the only foreigner there. After we took off, an African man looked at me with confusion in his eyes and asked, "Where are you going?"

I told him I was flying to the refugee camps of Adjumani.

He responded, "Don't you know that the American embassy has banned Americans from traveling to this region?"

I said I did not know this, but that I was traveling with Sudanese friends and I believed God would protect us because we were going to help the refugees in their struggle to survive. He responded with a smile and thanked me for the courage to go.

My Sudanese friend told me he did not know how we would get to the village where he was taking me since we were landing on a dirt grass runway about 30 miles from where we needed to go. He was taking me to the community he first went to when he fled Sudan. Not long after his arrival at that camp, he had started a church.

I asked him, "Are there any taxis at the airport where we will land?"

He replied, "No taxis, but God will lead us."

"What about buses we can take to get to the camp at Adjumani?" I asked.

"No buses," he replied, "but God will lead us."

I was beginning to imagine us walking for hours. What if we get stuck in the middle of the bush in Africa? What if the local LRA (Ugandan rebels) attacks us? I began to sense a strong fear within me. I began to pray and opened up the Scripture for guidance. I remembered what God said to Joshua, "Have I not commanded you? Be strong and courageous. Do not be terrified; do not be discouraged, for the Lord your God will be with you wherever you go." (Joshua 1:9)

When we landed there were only about a half dozen vehicles in sight, all belonging to non-government organizations. The people piled off the plane quickly! They got into their vehicles and took off. Then the African man who had spoken with me on the plane came up to me and asked, "Do you need a ride to Adjumani? I will take you and your friend."

After helping push the plane out of the mud, we all loaded up and headed off on a dirt road to our destination. The lush greenery was overwhelming! We soon approached a river and I realized that there was no bridge to take us across. One of the men told me, "We have come to the Nile, but the ferry workers are not working today so we must cross by canoe."

The Nile! So beautiful and bold, I had only seen the Nile in Cairo. We all waited and then two African men in a small dugout canoe came rowing up to the shore. It was so small I really didn't think we could fit. I got in and they handed me my bag and then handed me a small, tied up calf to place beside me; then a small bicycle. Pretty soon, I could not move an inch. The water came right to the edge of our little canoe and I knew I was about to go swimming down the Nile that day. I was certain the baby cow tied up next to me was going to start kicking. My fears proved unfounded, however, as we eventually made it across the Nile without incident.

Hours later, we finally arrived at the small village. The villagers greeted us by dancing and singing. It was a really an emotional time. We all watched as one group at a time began worshiping God by marching and singing into the small church made of grass. First, the children all dressed in their finest indigenous clothing went singing and marching into the church, with several other groups following. The last group was the elders and older adults. I finally got to go in, but discovered I could not enter the building to hear the indigenous instruments and singing because there was simply no room!

I truly have to say it was a taste of Glory! The children were all running around half naked and with bloated stomachs and smiles across their faces. After the service I asked the local pastor what the average offering was and he told me it was less than one U.S. dollar. So there we were, in the middle of a refugee camp with a local church of about 250 people who would probably never possess the means to travel throughout Africa or other parts of the world. Most were malnourished and living on United Nations handouts, but there was something powerful they possessed—a deep hunger and love for God. As I was leaving the church after spending most of the day there, I noticed a sign nailed to a tree. It read, "Adjumani Church: The Center for Global Impact and World Evangelization."

Imagine, a church with little resources and people who are all refugees and who will probably never leave their village during their lifetime, possessing something that is close to the heart of God—a passion and a vision for all the world to know and to worship God.

In America, it's common to drive by a church building and say, "Look at that church." Yes, that is a church building, but it is not the Church. The Church is people. I preached my first sermon to a Church when I was 16 years old while standing under a tree in Malawi, Africa. Some may argue that I was at a "preaching point" or an "outreach post." To me, that Church, on that particular day simply met under a tree and they were the body of Christ in that place.

The Growth of the Church

The church has grown more in the 20th Century than in all the previous 19 centuries since the time of Christ combined, with almost 2 billion adherents worldwide.[1] The current number of 81 million believers in China is expected to swell to 135 million by 2025. The 50 million faithful in India could mushroom to 125 million by 2050. Today's census of 90 million Christians in Africa is likely to explode to 1 billion by 2050.[2]

Today, around the world there are:

- 3.45 million local churches in the world—only 8 percent of these in North America.
- 33, 800 Christian denominations in the world.
- 23,000 para-church or service organizations.
- 4,100 foreign mission sending organizations.
- 1 million full-time ordained clergy (8 percent women).[3]

Indeed, for those who think that as Americans we are the only laborers left to fulfill the Great commission of our Lord, these statistics are both humbling and encouraging. We must explore new methods and models of partnering, collaborating and converging with our brothers and sisters in other nations to carry out the Great Commission across the globe.

The "Indigenous" Advantage

We decided to go on a two-day rafting trip in Nepal for a mere eight dollars. "How can we pass this up!" I said to my friend. We were young, hungry for adventure and on a limited budget, so this was definitely our kind of trip—especially since it included all food, camping gear, transportation and guides. After arriving at the Trissuli River in Nepal, we set off for hours of soaking in the beauty of the Himalayas. It was my first time rafting and I was beyond thrilled. I'm a sucker for adrenaline.

A few hours into the journey, we came upon a big rock that sucked us right in and tipped over our raft. I didn't mind; in fact, I was ready to go swimming! However, the water was more powerful than it looked. After a bit of struggle, I finally found the raft but I was worried about my Indian friend, Albert. You see, Albert didn't know how to swim. We had actually tried to talk him out of going with us because he did not know how to swim, but he was determined to share in the adventure, so we let him come.

Albert made it through the mishap all right, but he reacted to the experience quite differently from the rest of us! Later that evening several of us were sitting around the campfire discussing what had happened and thanking God for watching over us. Albert, meanwhile, was off to the side talking with four other Nepalis, all of them seated together inside a raft. I took a photo of them talking and it is still one of the most treasured photos I have today. Some time later, I asked Albert what he was talking about to those guys and he told me they come from the mountain villages and he had never heard their language. They were Newari and come from a low caste. There are over 70 languages and dialects spoken in Nepal, and many of them overlap. Albert spoke several languages himself: English, Nepali, Hindi, Bengali and Bhojpuri.

"I figured out their language as we were talking and began to talk to them about the Gospel," he told me. "They had never heard of Jesus Christ, so I told them how I almost died in the water, but how my God saved me because He takes care of His children. They were amazed that I would even talk to them because I come from a high caste."

What amazed me about his story was that it took him only minutes to communicate the Gospel to these men in their own language—in a way a westerner most likely could never have done. My view of world evangelization began shifting that evening by the camp fire.

Growing up in America, I had always heard how America was going to "win the world to Christ!" Perhaps it was not said exactly like this, but the idea was certainly strongly communicated in the way missions were talked about and done. Of course, I'm talking about my particular childhood denomination, but others, I'm sure, say the same thing. We as the church in the West have been guilty of thinking *we* alone will evangelize the world with our big budgets, large programs and great strategic ideas

To this day, the church in America still approaches missions with a blatantly Western idealism and a business model of doing international mission work. We analyze the "markets." We sell our "good and services." As James Engel and William Dyrness point out, "This western and contemporary missions' understanding is too often captive to American cultural realities, associating the Gospel with economic and political pragmatism."[4]

Many Americans still say things like, "Don't invest in nationals, they may steal your money," or "Nationals can't do it alone without the technology of the West," or "The nationals are not trained well enough to be able to reach their own people for Christ."

Well, don't mention China to someone who thinks like this! China's unregistered church has hardly been touched by the West, yet has grown tremendously without our technology, money or training. The way the world is going to be evangelized is through the *whole church*— not just the American church—taking the whole Gospel to the whole person all around the world.

Clearly, the way we approach global ministry in North America needs to change. Webster's defines paradox as, "A statement that is seemingly absurd or contradictory, yet is, in fact, true." Perhaps it is a paradox to say that we as westerners can make the most impact overseas by taking a back seat and working through local church communities that are indigenous to a particular region. After all, these people know their culture and language. They live at the same standard of living, and face the same daily struggles as the souls they are trying to reach.

I was visiting a western missionary in India and he told me he had to leave because his kids did not like the culture and they were having a hard time as a family. I know God used this missionary family, but their story caused me to lament over the huge amount of resources and energy it took to place them on the mission field, even though the success rate of them—and others like them—staying long-term is not really high.

It is estimated that it costs about $100,000 each year for a missionary family to be on the mission field overseas. It does not sadden me that westerners go overseas, but it saddens me when I hear stories of how their work is forced to stop because of cultural problems, political unrest, natural disasters and the like. I know this is not the case for all western missionaries. Many do a good job of working themselves out of a job by empowering the indigenous community. Yet, the simple fact is that indigenous missionaries do not leave their homes if a civil conflict breaks out or they have family problems. Why? Because their mission field *is their home*. I have heard too many stories of western missionaries who have left the field because of civil war, the death of a loved one back home or marital strife.

Am I saying that western missionaries should not go into the world? Absolutely not! It is crucial to the way we understand and live the Gospel that we send our own "sons and daughters" into the world to share the Good

News. The Great Commission is a command for all Christians throughout the world no matter how large or small the church is or what country it calls home. In fact, my family and I are living in Nepal now, so how could I advocate that western missionaries not answer the call to go into the world? I believe that we, as the western church, do play a crucial role in world evangelization. And yet, the western church simply cannot accomplish the task on its own.

For example, here in Nepal I recently read that 30 American Peace Corps volunteers had been forced to leave their district following an ultimatum by an armed group of Maoists. The Maoists—who hold a negative attitude toward Americans—demanded that the volunteers leave their region within six days. But even if the Americans had been allowed to stay, they would still have to leave eventually.

In Nepal, expatriates are only allowed to stay in the country for 10 years and may not stay beyond age 65. With this reality, which is similar to so many other places in the world, we simply cannot "go it alone" as westerners in our efforts to reach the world for Christ. To genuinely fulfill the Great Commission, we have no choice but to work with and through local believers to plant churches and do ministry to the poor and marginalized. Of course I realize that such cooperative relationships are not always possible, especially in unreached communities or cities where very few if any Christians live. I understand this reality and have faced it many times. But in general, interdependence is healthy in cross-cultural mission work—in whatever way that is expressed. To carry out the Great Commission effectively, we need interdependent relationships with other believers around the world just as surely as we need the power of the Holy Spirit.

Our mission started with a children's home and orphanage in north India in 1997. It is run by local, indigenous staff. The region of India where the home is located is very hostile to Christians, even if they are Indian. One local Hindu man would often send his child plus a few other children to throw rocks at the children who gathered every evening to sing worship songs. Thankfully, the facility is enclosed so there is no way for the stones to hit the children.

After doing this for several months, this Hindu man approached our Indian Director and said, "I have noticed you have come here and that you are an educated man. I was surprised by your presence here and did not understand why you came to this poor place. However, I see that you walk everywhere you go and, therefore, I am convinced that you are a holy man. I sent my son to throw stones at your children singing to your God, but I now want to send him to be a part of your day school program."

In India when a person walks everywhere he goes, he is revered and respected as a holy man. All Hindu priests and Sadus (Hindu holy men) walk wherever they go.

By contrast, if I lived in this region, I would want an SUV and all the things I thought I needed to "reach people for Christ." But when you work through the indigenous communities, you work according to their culture, gifts and way of doing things. Western missionaries can adjust and adapt to different aspects of the culture they are living and working in. But if I have to choose between having someone local, preaching the Gospel or a foreigner, preaching the Gospel, I will always choose the indigenous person, even if the foreigner is a "better" preacher. Why? Because in most of the regions of the world where the Gospel has not taken root and grown, the vast majority of the people perceive

Christianity as a "white man's" religion that is only of interest to westerners. To work apart from the indigenous church in any area of the world is simply not the wisest thing to do.

Of course, if there are no indigenous believers in a particular region, or if their numbers are very small, you many have to go it alone for a time, or else work in cooperation with Christians in a neighboring region or country where the Christian population is larger. But wherever it is possible, I believe that partnering directly with the indigenous church is the most effective way to further the Gospel.

Some might respond by saying, "Well, we cannot work with the indigenous church because they do not believe the right thing or do the right things like they need to." My response is simple: How often does God look at us as His children and say, "You do not do the right thing or believe the right thing, but I still work through you." God does not give up on us and He is patient with us. Therefore, we must adopt the same attitude with all of God's children across the globe who are our fellow laborers in Christ.

In Paul's letter to the church in Colossae, he mentions his friend Tychicus and calls him a fellow servant in the Lord. (Colossians 4:7) The Greek term translated "fellow servant" in this passage is *sundoulos* (soon'-doo-los), and means "a co-slave—a servitor or ministrant of the same master."[5] Paul is saying that he is equal to this man as a fellow slave of the same master. And so we are also to other followers of Jesus Christ. We are co-slaves of Christ, laboring together to see God's Kingdom come and God's will be done on earth as it is in heaven.

Allow me to share an example of what I mean. One year while in a southern region of the Philippines called Mindanao (where over 5 million Muslims live), I was staying with a Philipino missionary. One day while having lunch with an American missionary, I asked him about the large local Muslim community and asked him to take me to the villages where they live. He replied, "No, I cannot take you to the Muslim areas. They do not welcome me as an American."

I was shocked and discouraged. The next day, my Philipino missionary friend drove me right inside the Muslim village on the back of his motorcycle. We sat with the chief of the village and some town leaders. They knew this Philipino man was a Christian.

That day I also learned that the local well was broken. The well supplied water to the entire village, but since it was out of commission, the villagers had to walk a few hundred yards to get their water from a dirty stream! I realized I needed to help with this immediate need, but wondered what I would really be able to do. I asked my Philipino friend what the problem was and he explained that the well had a broken part, and would cost about $45 to fix. I told him to tell the Muslim community that they would have the part the next day. Upon hearing the news, the leaders gathered the whole village to meet us. My Philipino friend got to his feet and, after telling them their well would soon be repaired, began to share how Jesus Christ is the *living water*.

The Fruit of the Church

I remember going to the Korea for the first time while I was in college. For any follower of Jesus, seeing the fervency of the Korean church in prayer is a humbling experience. The older airport in Seoul is closer to the heart of the city, and when you fly in at night you can see the city covered with little red neon crosses on the tops of the buildings. These crosses mark where either small groups of believers or large churches meet to worship. The red symbolizes the blood of Christ covering the city. It is an amazing site to see.

Today, South Korea is the second most sending nation in the world when it comes to missions—second only to the United States. In 1979, there were only about 79 missionaries from Korea, but today there is an estimated 12,000. One South Korean missionary commented, "There is a saying that when Koreans now arrive in a new place, they establish a church; the Chinese establish a restaurant; the Japanese, a factory."[6] The largest Methodist, Presbyterian and Assembly of God churches are located in South Korea. The largest church in the world is in Seoul: Yoido Full Gospel Church. With all their satellite campuses, it is estimated to be more than 800,000 people strong. In their main building alone, more than 100,000 gather every weekend to worship God.

As you look at the amazing growth of the church in places like Korea and all around the world, there is great reason to rejoice. But there is also a need to ask ourselves some important questions. One of the most important is, "What is the church producing? Are we really producing disciples as Jesus instructed us to do?"

As Dallas Willard asks, "Have we inserted an omission in the Great Commission?"—meaning, are we actually "making disciples" as Jesus commanded us to do in Matthew 28:19-20 or are we making something else?

In Rwanda, during the mid 1990s, a great genocide occurred in which some 800,000 people died. If you research Rwanda, you will see that at the time of this travesty the nation was statistically more than 80 percent Christian. If that 80 percent had truly been trained and nurtured to become mature disciples of Jesus, I can't help but wonder if that terrible genocide could have been avoided.

Even today, some mission organizations don't consider Rwanda in their strategic planning because they say the country already has such a high percentage of professing Christians. But have those Christians received the discipleship training they need to become mature, effective followers of Christ? The central issue, as I see it, is that our missionary efforts should not be reduced solely to proclamation and evangelism, but should also focus on whole life transformational discipleship. After all, we are not commanded to make converts; we are commanded to make disciples.

As one African Christian leader said to a group of western missionaries, "You missionaries brought us Christ but you never taught us how to live."[7]

In order for transformational discipleship to happen, much of the church around the world needs encouragement and training. That training can come from many different places, not just the western church.

Churches in every culture around the world share at least one important question in common: Is it more important to fill up your church, or to equip your people to leave your church for ministry? From the perspective of many western churches, the easy answer will always be both, of course. But if you look at our western churches' priorities—how money is spent or decisions made—you will usually discover that the answer is different from what we say.

Surely, the mistake the church makes is focusing more on getting people inside the four walls and meeting their "needs," instead of equipping them for ministry out in the world. As Brian McLaren says, "In my thinking, church doesn't exist for the benefit of its members. It exists to equip its members for the benefit of the world...We don't recruit people to be customers of our products or consumers of our religious programs; we recruit them to

be colleagues in our mission. The church doesn't exist to
satisfy the consumer demands of believers; the church
exists to equip and mobilize men and women for God's
mission in the world."[8] The mission of the church must
include *both* introducing the Gospel to people and growing
people in the Gospel. Both tasks are equally important.
But both are rarely done.

In the teaching I do with untrained pastors around
the developing world, I often address this issue and ask
them which task they believe is the most important. I will
often have them raise their hands to indicate their choice.
Most of the time they do not know how to respond, and
think it is an either/or answer. Then I tell the following
old story to illustrate the need within the church to do
both:

There was once a wise old teacher who held up a
glass of water and asked the age old question to the young
pupil, "What do you see? Is the glass half full or half
empty?"

The pupil said to his teacher, "It depends whether
you are filling it up, or pouring it out."

The teacher asked his pupil, "Well, what are you
doing the most?"

The pupil responded, "I believe I am constantly
doing both."

The wise teacher replied, "It has been revealed to
you the purpose of the glass!"

Gathered to be Scattered

The purpose of the church is to both fill up and to
pour out. It is the gathering of people for worship,
sacrament, teaching and community so they can be sent
out to demonstrate and proclaim the love of God in their
community and the entire world. Unfortunately, churches
in the West are usually best known for the first aspect

(bringing people in), but rarely for the second (sending disciples out). You can probably name several churches in your area that are good at bringing people in their doors but poor at sending them out fully equipped to serve their communities and the world. This simply should not be! Every church's vision should carry global implications because God always has a global agenda and vision.

I love cafeterias. My friends always make fun of me for delighting in an establishment where most of the time you feel like you are stepping into a retirement home. Okay, I realize that many seniors frequent cafeterias, but *I really like them.* My wife always makes fun of me, too

In a cafeteria, it's fun to watch children try to pick out what they want instead of what their parents want for them. I remember seeing a family that had to leave because their little son was so upset because he could not have Jell-O. He went crazy in the middle of the line and his parents were too embarrassed to stay, discipline him and enjoy their meal. I often wonder what it would be like if children could simply pick out their own meal at a cafeteria without interference from Mom or Dad. Their tray would look something like this: two Jell-O's, chocolate milk, ice cream, pudding and a cinnamon roll. If they ate like this all the time, they would certainly be malnourished, hyperactive, and overweight from such a horrible diet. And yet, this is exactly how many people in the church are nourished spiritually. We choose what feels good, tastes good and looks good. Consequently, what have we produced as the church in America is a lot of malnourished, hyper, bored and fat Christians!

Surely, this is the mistake of the church in many regions of the world. But within my heritage, the West, it is especially true. It is always a sad reality to hear of churches that wait 10 or 20 years before they begin a global missions ministry within their community. They believe reaching out solely to their own community is the entire calling of their church. Most would not admit this, but their priorities, emphases and budgets clearly reflect it. What a mistake and tragedy this is.

This is poor discipleship and a weak decision. Actively participating in God's global purposes is something every church should do, right from the very first day of its existence. This is not only wise, but good theology as God is a "missionary God" who desires worshipers from all nations and tribes. Acts 1:8 clearly says that outreach and ministry from a local church should simultaneously target our own city (Jerusalem) our local region (Judea), the larger region (Samaria), and other areas across the globe (uttermost parts of the world).

The Gospel and Life Transformation

Once while I was in Africa, I had opportunity to talk to an African Bible scholar and missionary. He said to me, "Many Christian leaders and Bible scholars in the western world have made a great mistake by separating everything in the Christian life. If you want to know a cat, you don't cut up the cat and study its different parts in separate pieces. Instead, you live with the cat and come to know it."

Many surveys have been done that describe how there is not much difference between church people and non-church people in the West when it comes to giving to the poor, divorce rate and honesty in business affairs. Why do you suppose that is?

The word "disciple" is used 297 in the Bible. The word Christian is used three. Should this tell us something? Has the church been more concerned about "decisions" or "converts" than it is about making people authentic followers of Jesus, committed to living as "students" of Jesus throughout their entire lives?

The philosopher, Soren Kierkergaard said the church is filled with "the admirers of Jesus," but not many followers. For too long we have allowed ourselves to be satisfied with churches full of people who are merely cultural Christians or admirers of Jesus and who have never had their lives transformed by the power of the Gospel. Being a follower of Jesus means we are to be transformed into His likeness

The Bible says, "But whenever anyone turns to the Lord, the veil is taken away. Now the Lord is the Spirit, and where the Spirit of the Lord is, there is freedom. And we, who with unveiled faces all reflect the Lord's glory, are being transformed into his likeness with ever-increasing glory, which comes from the Lord, who is the Spirit."[9]

The goal of the Christian disciple is not information but transformation. To be transformed means to change the character, form or appearance of something else. This is what the Gospel does. It changes us. I am not talking about mere external changes such as the style of clothing we wear, our tastes in the arts, or the way we talk. The Gospel changes our very soul, so that our motives, attitudes and intentions come to reflect Jesus Christ to the world.

I like what Rick Warren writes about this, "God's ultimate goal for your life on earth is not comfort, but character development. He wants you to grow up spiritually and become like Christ. Becoming like Christ does not mean losing your personality or becoming a mindless clone. God created your uniqueness, so He certainly does not want to destroy it. Christ-likeness is all about transforming your character, not your personality."[10]

It is commonly known that Dr. B.R Ambedker, the father of the Indian Constitution, was at one time interested in embracing Christ. In 1956 he was asked,

"Which religion does not oppress people?" The question inspired him to find an answer. He studied Hinduism, Buddhism and Christianity, and came to the conclusion that Christianity was the only one that taught equality. He was ready to embrace the teachings of Jesus.

Then one day he went to a church where he found two communion stations. He asked a leader in the church, "Why are there two communion stations?" The church leader responded, "One is for the high caste and the other for the low caste." He was greatly disturbed by this, and eventually decided to embrace Buddhism instead. What a lost opportunity for the Gospel in India!

Even the great Mahatmas Gandhi was once kicked out of a church in England while he was there pursuing his studies. He responded to the affront by saying, "I thought Christianity teaches love. This is not love."

Oftentimes the church does not display or teach the Christ of the Bible who taught equality and love. The reality is that the church today is filled with people who have not been transformed into the image of Jesus Christ but are merely going through religious ritual.

Perhaps the root of the problem is that we have made the Gospel too easy or too comfortable for too long for too many people in the church. We have allowed people to hear the Gospel over and over with no visible commitment to see their lives transformed into Christ-likeness.

Yes, we are patient with people, but perhaps we are too tolerant of people who do not really want to follow Jesus Christ with their whole lives. Gordon Cosby of the Church of the Savior in Washington, D.C. says, "We must come to the place where we can do what Jesus did, where we can watch the rich young ruler walk away and, with sorrow and an ache in our hearts, let him go until he can come back on the terms of Jesus Christ. We have been so afraid we might lose potential members that we have been willing to take them on their own terms. Then we wonder why the church is relatively impotent and doesn't have the power to transform human life, to shake society to its very roots."[11]

Destroying the Success Syndrome

We are preoccupied with numbers and the trappings of success in America—both as individuals and church communities. But that kind of success is not a value of the Kingdom of God. Jesus left the future of the Gospel in the hands of ordinary men who by western standards would probably not be defined as "successful people." Most of them were uneducated and poor and none of them had any qualifications to be leaders of God's church. Except one, that is.

Yet, they had *all* been with Jesus.

Many churches often ask the wrong questions in hiring leaders to shepherd their people. "What is your education? What is your salary requirement?"

I seldom hear questions like, "What kind of integrity and character does this person have? What are his/her key relationships like? How well does he/she love and serve others? Does he/she walk with Jesus?"

Of course, we should always strive to serve God with our best, but we must also abandon this obsession with measuring our success in the church by numbers alone. We as individuals and churches should strive to grow in Kingdom values and not merely in numerical, quantifiable ways. Signs of growth in Kingdom values include a deeper communion with God, authentic and honest community with our brothers and sisters in Christ, a growing capacity to love the unlovable, and a deepening desire to give more generously of our time, treasures and talents in order to build God's Kingdom.

Henri Nouwen wrote, "We have been called to be fruitful—not successful, not productive, not accomplished. Success comes from strength, stress and human effort. Fruitfulness comes from vulnerability and the admission of our own weakness."

Who Cares About the Structure?

When should an adjective be inserted before the word "church" to define who the church is? I think we should be careful using adjectives to define our churches. So many want to define their church by inserting "house, seeker, postmodern, mega or organic" before the word church to broadcast the church's style or structure to the world. Of course, I understand that descriptive words are sometimes needed to distinguish between the different models and ways that church is done. But very often these words only serve to distract believers away from God's core purpose for the church. We get so busy "being" postmodern or mega or seeker that we forget our true goal—becoming like Jesus and sharing His message of love with the world.

These descriptive labels can also tend to foster division between different churches in a community or region. Many who use these "defining adjectives" make the bold claim that their particular form or structure for the church is the "best" or "only" way church can be done. But the church is more than any one structure or any one particular style.

The word "church" comes from the Greek word, *ecclesia* and its meaning is broad and simple: "Calling out, i.e. (concretely) a popular meeting, especially a religious congregation."[12] There is room for great diversity and multiple models within the body of Christ. In fact, such diversity is essential if we are to reach the world for Christ. We must come to embrace that fact. Churches that meet in houses, 500-year-old cathedrals or modern school cafeterias are all valid. Churches that enjoy old organs, electric guitars or a sitar should all exist. Some churches may choose to gather large crowds of people and create smaller groups out of that, while others emphasize only the small groups themselves.

The core issues of a healthy, vibrant church are not rooted in the organizational structure or style of music but in the character qualities of its people—qualities like humility, integrity, brokenness, holiness, love, authenticity and patience. So embrace the diversity of the body of Christ. Celebrate how Jesus is building His church today in so many different kinds of models and forms.

I arrived in Havana from Mexico City. My Cuban friends who were escorting me into Cuba got detained in Mexico City and never even made it to Cuba. So I arrived at the Havana airport without them—and a little confused about what I should do next. I knew I was to travel to another city on the island and had to board a train and ride it through the night. But I had no idea who to look for or who was going to meet me.

Arriving early in the morning at the train station, I walked around for about an hour hoping to find someone to help me. Then two older ladies who could not walk very well came in, pointed to me and said my name. We walked outside and they gestured for me to hop into the back of a wagon being pulled by two horses. I did.

As we began going down the brick roads, I said to myself, "Here I am being led by these two grandmothers, and I have no idea who they are or where I am going!" I saw people getting up in the early morning, sweeping their front porches and getting ready for the day. Finally, we arrived at a home where a pastor was there to greet us. I actually forgot that it was Sunday. He asked me to preach in his church in just two hours. Grateful for the opportunity, I agreed.

Being at that church that morning was an amazing experience. The building was only half finished. People stood outside and did not have a seat. The sound system did not work. Despite these things, the church was filled with life and an authentic expression that would draw anyone looking into the claims of Jesus. There was laughter and joy and a true spirit of brokenness at the same time. It was an amazing time of being with a church.

If you ever have the privilege of visiting a church in oppressed regions of the world where there are few resources,s you will often find several common themes among them. One major theme is that the church does not exist solely for itself but is committed to worshiping God and being the body of Christ to the community, no matter what the cost. They live simple lives and are not bound to materialism. They integrate both evangelism and social action and don't think of it as separate ministries. They offer help when someone is in need, such as paying a neighbor's electric bill or providing care for each other's children. They are concerned about other nations knowing who Jesus Christ is. They seem to meet together all the time to pray. They love to sing to God and to give thanks for who He is and all that He has done.

They don't really care what time they get out of church and hardly look at their watches during the sermon. They give more than 25 to 35 percent of their income away to the church and the poor. They care for the orphans and widows in their own communities. Surely this is the only model for the church that Jesus would have us all follow!

So I say let the church be the church—in all its multiple expressions and forms—and let it be transformed into the image of Christ and empowered by the Holy Spirit to move out into the world to demonstrate and proclaim the hope that is ours.

Questions for Personal Reflection or Small Group Study:

1. In what ways have you been encouraged to believe that we, as westerners, will be the only ones to win the world to Christ? Do you agree with this? How can you help influence this idea, which many western Christians have?

2. What can you do to help educate yourself on the growth of the body of Christ in the world?

3. What does partnership in ministry mean to you, whether locally or globally?

4. Why do we need each other as the body of Christ throughout the world?

5. Can you think of a time when you experienced the church not reflecting Christ's love? How did you deal with it?

Notes

1. *A Comparative Survey of Churches and Religions in The Modern World* (Second Edition), edited by David B. Barrett, George T. Kurian and Todd M. Johnson (New York, 2001), 19 and 551

2. *A Comparative Survey of Churches and Religions in The Modern World* (Second Edition), 405ff

3. *World Christian Encyclopedia* (Two Volumes), edited by D.B. Barrett, G.T. Kurian and T.M. Johnson (Oxford University Press, 2001)

4. *James F.Engel and William A. Dyrness,* Changing the Mind of World Missions: Where Have We Gone Wrong? *(Intervarsity Press, Downers Grove, IL, 2000), 18*

5. *Biblesoft's New Exhaustive Strong's Numbers and Concordance with Expanded Greek-Hebrew Dictionary* (Biblesoft and International Bible Translators, Inc, 1994)

6. Norimitsu Onishi, "Faith & Values: Korean export—salvation," *New York Times*, November 27, 2004

7. *Changing the Mind of Missions: Where Have we Gone Wrong*, 22

8. Brian D. McLaren, *A New Kind of Christian* (Jossey-Bass Inc., San Francisco, CA, 2001)

9. 2 Corinthians 3:16-18

10. Rick Warren, *The Purpose Driven Life* (Zondervan, Grand Rapids, MI; 2002), 171

11. As quoted in "The Journey Inward, Outward, and Forward" by Jeff Bailey, Vineyard USA, Cutting Edge Newsletter, Fall 2001

12. *Biblesoft's New Exhaustive Strong's Numbers and Concordance with Expanded Greek-Hebrew Dictionary* (Biblesoft and International Bible Translators, Inc, 1994)

CHAPTER
2

Being the Good News People

"Not all who wander are lost."—J.R.R. Tolkien

"Perhaps if there were more of that intense distress for souls that leads to tears, we should more frequently see the results we desire. Sometimes it may be that while we are complaining of the hardness of the hearts of those we are seeking to benefit, the hardness of our own hearts and our feeble apprehension of the solemn reality of eternal things may be the true cause of our want of success."—J. Hudson Taylor

*"Preach the gospel everyday; if necessary, use words."
—Francis of Assisi*

*"His authority on earth allows us to dare to go to all the nations. His authority in heaven gives us our only hope of success. And His presence with us leaves us no other choice."
—John R. W. Stott*

Fear. It is something we all experience and live with on different levels. The fears of growing up, being alone, getting married, having no money, going to college, growing old or dying are common to us all. Has anyone ever asked you what the first emotion recorded in the Bible is? It is fear. Adam was fearful and hid from God. In Genesis 3:10 Adam said to God, "I was afraid because I was naked, so I hid myself." Is there a reason why fear is recorded as the first emotion in the Bible? Could it be that God is trying to tell us something about the condition of humanity?

I believe fear is what keeps us from being who God wants us to be and doing what God wants us to do. Some fear is good. I want my son to have some fear in him when he approaches a busy street. Yet, unhealthy fear is like chains wrapped around our ankles and attached to a large weight. It keeps us from moving forward and growing, progressing and maturing. Fear may keep us from loving others because of what they may think of us. Fear keeps us from pursuing God with our whole hearts because of the change that such a commitment may really entail.

Beyond all this, fear keeps us, the people of God, from becoming together what we can never be alone as individuals. Often people outside the church see Christians as not loving each other but rather being quick to point out our differences and diversity of approaches in ministry. Perhaps it is fear that keeps us from loving those who are different from us within the Christian family. It is easy to be around only those who look like us, have the same political view as we do, and share the same economic background. But is *that* the sort of church God desires?

Jesus responded in a profound way to the fear of the disciples in John 20. After He was crucified on the cross, the disciples locked themselves in a room for fear of the Jews. (verse 19) They had given their lives to Jesus and were now thinking that their teacher and master had abandoned them and they were to be killed next. But Jesus appeared in their midst and said, "Peace be with you." (verse 19) Upon seeing Jesus, I am sure the disciples were set free from their fear. Jesus then revealed Himself to the disciples to remove all doubt (verse 20) and said a second time, "Peace be with you; as the Father has sent me, I also am sending you." The words of Jesus here speak of sending the disciples on a mission. The word "mission" does not appear in the Bible, but surely this Scripture is what "missions" is all about. The Father sends the Son. The Son sends the Spirit. The Triune God sends all of us who walk with Jesus into a lost and dark world to make disciples of all nations.

Jesus wants to respond to our fear today just as He responded to the fear of His disciples. Surely, Jesus wants to be present in the midst of our fear; He wants to speak to us and reveal Himself to us. Jesus said, "My sheep hear my voice, and I know them, and they follow me."[1]

As a teenager, I began hearing the voice of Jesus telling me to go and preach the Gospel to peoples and nations that do not live in the lap of luxury like that which surrounded me as a kid in suburbia America. School was over, and I was looking forward to summer, just as any other teenager was. I had just finished my sophomore year in high school and had no homework or classes for three months. Sleeping in, going out with friends at night, having parties, going to summer camp—these were the things high school kids live for, right?

Not me. I wanted something more. I was pursuing God and wanted to talk to everyone about God. During that formative time of my life, something mystical and transcendent happened that made me want to follow God with my whole heart. I don't remember it being one event or one specific prayer. Rather, it was God working through everything I experienced or thought to draw me to Himself.

Following Jesus was all I could think about at 16. Jesus Christ was not just a historical figure or an image I saw on jewelry—but He was alive, active and pursuing my heart. "Did God choose me or did I choose him?" some would ask and even get into a theological argument over. Who really knows? All I know is Jesus Christ became real and alive to me that summer and I wanted to tell everyone. So I did!

I began to understand that Jesus was a person who lived on earth and was God in the flesh. He lived in a different period of time, yet faced many of the same issues all humans face: fear, doubt, pain, disappointment, sorrow, joy, laughter and sickness. I did face a bit of a dilemma though; I did not feel I had a dramatic story like I heard others share. I had no "gutter to glory" story. I had not been real rebellious before coming to Christ. I had no prison time, no history with drugs, no getting "slammed out of my mind" every weekend. I thought I should probably go do all that kind of stuff so I could really have a story to tell; then more people would understand the power of the Gospel to change you and give you hope, security and meaning in life.

Luckily, I realized this was a lie from hell and chose to simply continue to follow Jesus with my whole heart. In those early years, I went out and witnessed at concerts, carnivals, football games—anywhere I could. A "fool" I probably was, but also a "fool" who did not care what others thought of me.

A tragic experience and a high school friend, Brian, really impacted me. Our brief relationship in many ways began a deep compassion for those who do not know God. Brian confessed to a group of us skiing in Colorado that he did not know God and he would end up in hell if he died. I remember feeling overwhelmed that someone would have that thought. Later we got together to talk. Sadly, he denied the claims of Christ and did not want to receive Jesus Christ as his Lord. After we returned home, Brian held a shotgun to his face and ended his life.

The thought of him entering into a Christless eternity was more than I could handle. I don't know if he ever came to Christ before his suicide; only God knows, but the thought that millions of people in the world are without God and who look at life and death without hope was more than I could handle. Suddenly, I had a cause I wanted to give my life to. I wept for days and could not hold in the pain I felt in my heart for people who did know God. Perhaps other people had been praying for me to develop a heart and a love for God and for people. I don't know, but God heard their prayers. Whatever the circumstances were that led to the opportunity for me to go to overseas that first time, it was God who designed it.

The trip was organized at my home church where the door was opened for a small team to travel to Malawi, Africa. I remember when I told my friends where I was going, I got strange looks back from them. "Why would you want to go there?" they asked. I didn't care what others thought or said. I remember reading where Jesus told His disciples, "As the Father has sent me, I also am sending you." I also read, "How, then, can they call on the one they have not believed in? And how can they believe in the one of whom they have not heard? And how can they hear without someone preaching to them? And how can they preach unless they are sent?"[2] Through God's Spirit and His word, I was filled with boldness and did not care what my peers thought of my decision.

I could not sleep for several nights before our departure in anticipation of what was to come. My first international flight was about to happen! When we made a connection in Amsterdam, I was told that I had a new seat on the nine-hour flight down to Africa. When I got on the plane, I realized I had a seat in first class. "Something is wrong, I don't think I should be sitting here," I told the flight attendant. She told me there was a mistake in the booking and I had gotten moved to first class. I could not believe it. My first "overseas mission" and I was flying first class. They actually used real eggs to make me scrambled eggs! I remember saying to God, "God, I will go to any country in the world for you if I can fly like this!"

Well, little did I know at 16 how God did hear my prayer and how my life would unfold in the years to come (though not the part about always flying first class!).

Stepping out of the airport in Malawi, my first thought was, "I want to move here and live." I was like a kid going to the amusement park for the first time and discovering rides I had never imagined. The smells, the architecture, the sounds, and sights were all new to me. Little did I know how this first reaction would change how I was to live my life. I was overwhelmed. I saw a boy chewing what appeared to be a stick. I made the comment too soon, "The people are so hungry here they're eating sticks." The missionary quickly corrected me and told me he was eating sugar cane. I immediately told him, "I want some of that."

In the days that followed we worked with a few local churches and schools. Then one day I was asked to preach at a local church. "What will I say?" I asked. "I am only 16 and I will be speaking through an interpreter!" I knew I would do it, but I still had doubts. *I will be speaking to so many people older than me,* I thought. *Can I do this?*

I remembered a verse I had shared with my youth group a few months before at the weekly youth gathering at our church. They were words Paul wrote to the younger Timothy: "Don't let anyone look down on you because you are young, but set an example for the believers in speech, in life, in love, in faith and in purity. Until I come, devote yourself to the public reading of Scripture, to preaching and to teaching."[3]

This empowered me and gave me the confidence I needed. *I can do this!* I thought. Mine wasn't like sermons I had watched others deliver. I got to do my first one under a tree and was the only white person for miles around. Shirtless mothers nursing their babies, chickens and goats roaming around, and children coming up to me in the middle of the service were all new experiences for me that day. It was actually natural to be able to speak through an interpreter because you could pause and think about what you were going to say next. I loved it. I remember preaching on Matthew 7:13-14, the narrow road and the wide road. As I asked the people sitting there if they wanted to walk on the narrow road and follow Jesus, several people committed their lives to Christ.

After the service I was taken to eat lunch and discovered that the house I was eating in was not like the other ones. This one actually had walls and was not a mud hut. Lunch was served and I found myself being the only white person in this whole village, and the village was outside watching and singing in my honor. I could not believe I was the only one from our small team. The others had received invitations from other churches. An African pastor, Bombo Chisi, was my host. I did not realize at the time but this experience and my time with this young, dynamic African young pastor would plant seeds in my heart and give me a love for the indigenous church around the world.

What an experience for a 16 year old—or for anyone for that matter! At the lunch, I began to notice something unusual was going on and asked my interpreter what was happening. He told me we were eating at the chief's house and that the chief was actually going to come and join us. I was confused and wondered why he was not already there, but I did not say anything.

I was having fun eating with my hands (as the locals did) and enjoying the new and different tastes. All of a sudden loud cheers came from outside. The chief arrived and I thought, *Wow! This guy must be a pretty important man around here.* We did the traditional African greeting by shaking hands in a special way and he sat down and began to eat. He soon asked me through the interpreter, "Why are you here?"

I told him I had come to see his beautiful country and the people who lived here and to tell people about Jesus Christ."

The mood changed and he got very quiet. He and the interpreter began to talk between each other and a small conversation began to move into what seemed to be an argument. I asked what was going on and my interpreter said the chief did not want me to talk about Jesus Christ anymore. In the midst of their conversation he slammed down his fist a few times in obvious anger. I didn't know what to think. But being compelled by the Holy Spirit, I told my interpreter that I wanted to tell the chief a few thoughts, if I could, before we left. I began to tell him what the Gospel meant to me as I understood it at that age, and I told him that it was not just an opinion of a youngster from America as he may think.

As the conversation continued, he slammed his fist down on the desk and began yelling at the interpreter and walked out of his own home. I could not believe it! Had I insulted a man in his own home? I began to get very afraid and began to wonder if I would ever make it out of there alive. He later came back in and talked to the pastor, who was his friend. We finished lunch and I played with his children. The chief was cordial to me as I left. After lunch, some local missionaries arrived in their van to pick me up. As you might imagine, I was glad to see them.

A few weeks later I was on a plane back to America. A few weeks after I arrived, I received a letter from my interpreter. He told me the chief I had met was not just the chief of that village but of more than 100 villages in that region. He was an important man and a well-known leader. He also told me he was very much against Christianity in his country and wanted it stopped. He wrote of problems the chief was causing for people in the villages he supervised who were Christians, how he was not treating them properly and making them pay more taxes.

For years, the interpreter and other Christian leaders had tried to share Christ with this chief. Many people were praying for him. At the end of the letter, he told me that after we left Malawi the chief embraced Christ and wanted to follow Him with his life and change his ways.

I was thrilled! In closing the letter, he said the chief remembered the day I had spoke about Christ at such a young age, and how I was not afraid to speak to such an important man so clearly and with confidence. The pastor from Malawi said he believed the Holy Spirit used that time to convict the chief in his process of coming to Christ.

As I reflect, even today, on that encounter many years ago, a verse in the Bible comes to mind, "God has chosen the foolish things of the world to confound the wise."[4]

You see, I was foolish and didn't even know what I said exactly at such a young age. But it is not important what I did or said. What matters is what God did through me as I made myself available. God wants not our ability but our availability to be used by Him, regardless of our age, our education, our vocation, ethnicity or possessions. God wants us to give our fears to Him and simply be available.

Have you ever heard these words from a good friend: "Guess what? Something amazing happened. I have to tell you about it!"? Whenever something good, important or meaningful happens to us, we immediately think about all the people we want to tell. You got a date for your high school prom, you made an A on a test, you got accepted at the college you like best, you met the person you want to marry, you landed the perfect job, you found out you were going to be a parent, you got venture capital to start your own business. Whatever it is, we all want to tell those closest to us what happened.

Jesus answered a skeptic who was searching for truth, saying, "I tell you the truth, no one can enter the kingdom of God unless he is born of water and the Spirit. Flesh gives birth to flesh, but the Spirit gives birth to spirit."[5]

Both as individuals and as local communities, we have the greatest and most beautiful treasure to share with the world. That treasure is the reality of the birth, death and resurrection of the Lord Jesus Christ. His death provides the forgiveness of sins: past, present and future. And this treasure and gift is available to all who confess and believe. Jesus Christ is the one who saves, changes and transforms us. All He asks us to do is share the Good News.

The Mystery of Salvation

The greatest gift we have in the world is the free gift of salvation through Christ. This basic reality, I have shared with people from all around the world. I have told many people from other religions that God has initiated relationship with us. The difference between Christianity and other faiths is that all other religions are based on people's efforts and works to lead them to God, Karma or to enlightenment. But the great news of the Gospel is God making the first move by sending Jesus Christ to earth. God demonstrates His love for us *first*, to show us that we do not have to do anything to deserve or earn God's love for us.

The basic premise of coming to Christ is something so glorious and beautiful that in reality it is sometimes difficult to put into words. But it is not a complicated thing. Jesus said we must become like a little child to enter the Kingdom of Heaven (Matthew 18:3). Indeed, faith in God comes easily for children.

Salvation that allows us to know God and have a home in heaven includes these qualities:

• **It is a mystery and working of the Holy Spirit**. Salvation is foundationally a work of the Holy Spirit. People often ask me, "Do you convert people?"

I say, "No." The Holy Spirit convicts and converts people, not our words or actions. In John 3, Jesus talks to a religious man who asks Him how to have eternal life. "I tell you the truth, no one can enter the Kingdom of God unless he is born of water and the Spirit. Flesh gives birth to flesh, but the Spirit gives birth to spirit. You should not be surprised at my saying, 'You must be born again.' The wind blows wherever it pleases. You hear its sound, but you cannot tell where it comes from or where it is going. So it is with everyone born of the Spirit."[6]

The Greek word for "Spirit" in this passage is *pneuma*. This word can be translated as "wind"—as in, "You don't know where the wind is blowing; so it is with the spirit of God, who allows this new birth to take place in people's hearts."

• **It is not by our own efforts or works**. "For it is by grace you have been saved, through faith—and this not from yourselves, it is the gift of God—not by works, so that no one can boast."[7] Salvation is free. We cannot buy it, earn it or inherit it. We cannot be a good enough person, go to religious venues enough, meditate enough, or perform religious duties enough to receive salvation. It is a gift from God.

• **It is solely by the Goodness, Grace and Love of God**. "But God demonstrates His own love for us in this: While we were still sinners, Christ died for us."[8] It is only by the grace and goodness of God that we can receive salvation. God saves us; we don't save ourselves. His love for us is too great to comprehend or imagine. There is no love as pure and real as God's love and He demonstrated it purely in Jesus Christ.

• **Jesus Christ is the sole means of salvation.** When you closely study the teachings of Jesus, you see the exclusively of His claims. He was not an inclusive teacher when it came to connecting with God. "Jesus answered, 'I am the way and the truth and the life. No one comes to the Father except through me.'"[9]

"Enter through the narrow gate. For wide is the gate and broad is the road that leads to destruction, and many enter through it. But small is the gate and narrow the road that leads to life, and only a few find it."[10] Knowing God can be found only in Jesus Christ. We cannot know the God of the Bible through other great teachers or gurus; only through Jesus Christ.

• **It is something we participate in throughout our entire life**. One of the misunderstandings people have when they come to Christ is that they think all you do is simply say a prayer and nothing more after that. Salvation is meant to be "worked out" through our whole lives, not to be earned, but to be grown and nurtured in the grace and knowledge of Jesus Christ. "Therefore, my dear friends, as you have always obeyed—not only in my presence, but how much more in my absence—continue to work out your salvation with fear and trembling, for it is God who works in you to will and to act according to his good purpose."[11] This process, called sanctification, means we are to become set apart and made holy, as Christ was holy. This will take our whole lives and we will never reach perfection until we reach heaven.

What Has Gone Wrong in Communicating the Good News?

The church's message is often not the message of Jesus at all. For example, a church may speak of a certain political ideology you must embrace in order to be included in the Kingdom of God. Some in the church even advocate "making Jesus your choice so you can drive a Rolls Royce." But did following Jesus have economic gain for the first century disciples? Not hardly. Sometimes the church speaks of certain cultural standards and rules that must be followed: "Don't do this," "Listen to that," "Dress like this," "Don't wear your hair like that," ...*then* you can have a relationship with Jesus. Such arbitrary requirements and unbiblical promises certainly do not reflect the true Gospel of Christ.

But even when the message of the Gospel is technically right, often the very way we share it robs it of its impact.

• **The medium distorts the message.** Sometimes the way the church proclaims the Good News of salvation is like hearing the most beautiful symphony through a transistor radio bought at a garage sale. So often how we communicate the Good News of Jesus does not do justice to the message itself.

If you ever get to travel, you often hear the English language spoken in very different ways—from rural Mississippi to the Bronx, to the Pacific Northwest to England, to Australia to a place where someone speaks English as a second language. Many times when you hear people speak English in a different way or in an accent, you don't really listen to *what* they say; just *how* they say it. Their tone, accent or drawl makes you focus on the way they are saying something instead of the content of their message.

What are we to say as individuals and as the church to people and cultures around us? Many people have a false perception or understanding of Jesus simply because of how the church has chosen to communicate Jesus. When many people think of Christianity, they picture a guy yelling on the street, the TV lady with her opulent jewelry, or a million other images come to their minds. The way Christians speak the truth without love or speak love without truth, is frustrating, confusing and damaging to the cause of Christ.

- **Selling a product.** So often the way we've been taught to share our faith comes across as a sales presentation. The goal is to "close the deal" and then move on to the next customer. I actually had a person who loves God and who is committed to service ask me once, "How do you close the deal?" I was shocked that committed Christians would think this way when it comes to sharing their faith.

We come as confident salespeople, having the goods, and we perceive our "sales target" as having no concept of faith, no experience with God revealing Himself to them, and no times of conviction by the Holy Spirit. It's as if we don't even suspect that Christ could have been working in their lives, opening their eyes to a measure of the truth long before we ever came on the scene. Who's to say they won't have something to teach us about faith or about God? His Spirit is at work everywhere, and in many people we may not even expect. Not just in us.

Augustine, who lived in the 5th Century, had a prayer I believe speaks to understanding how we should share our faith. "Lord, allow me to be with those who are seeking the truth, but deliver me from those who think they have found it."

None of us knows everything. We are not completely "there." We are not completely sanctified or holy, nor do we think and behave in godly ways 24/7. We strive for that, but we must also realize we are not there. We are to be honest and real. That is what Augustine's prayer means, and it should impact the way we share our faith.

Here are a few thoughts and suggestions on sharing your faith journey:

Share your faith while admitting you have much to learn on this journey called life. St. Francis of Assisi wrote, "Seek to understand rather than to be understood." Sharing your faith is not about controlling the conversation and telling someone what you know. In fact, so often our manner of communication destroys the message all together. Sharing your faith in the context of relationship—being honest and open about your own struggles and fears—is much more powerful than sharing how the other person needs to change. Some in the church identify those who come to faith as no longer being seekers. Instead, they identify only pre-Christ followers as "the seekers." This implies that after we have accepted Christ we are no longer seeking. Can't we still be seekers after coming to Christ? I believe we can be and should be. But in sharing our faith, we often do not come to people with this attitude. Be honest with others as you share your faith. Admit that you are still seeking Christ and want to understand who He is even more now than when you first accepted Him.

Share your faith in community. Faith journeys are not meant to be lived alone. Lesslie Newbigin, the famous missionary to India, has aptly described Christian community as *the interpretation of the Gospel*. Authentic Christian community embodies both the Gospel's message and its essence. We convey the Gospel to the world not only through what we say, but also through the vibrant life we share together in community.[12] We need redemption and we need a community of people to share it with. Inviting friends and family who perhaps are not followers of Jesus to come be a part of your Christian community is very fruitful. People should see how followers of Christ spend their money, relate to their spouses, encourage each other, share their possessions with each other in time of need (Acts 2:44-45), and never give up meeting together. (Hebrews 10:25) Some Christians harbor a "separatist" attitude that holds them back from building genuine community with people of non-faith. But this attitude is based in fear and has nothing to do with the Apostle John's admonition to keep ourselves from the enticements of this world. (1 John 2:15)

Share faith in service to your community and the world. A very strong way to allow lost people to engage with issues of the Gospel is to invite them to join your church in serving the poor in their own communities and around the world. Many times we have this idea that we need to get equipped, work out our problems, and prepare before we'll be ready to serve others effectively. I believe it's quite the opposite. It's in serving others that people realize how much they need God. Mission work, locally and globally, is not solely for the "mature Christian" of the church, but can provide an open door for the skeptic to choose to follow or return to Jesus. I have seen this first-hand many times and have heard many people tell stories of how the opportunity to build a house for the poor or encourage orphans was a key step in them coming to Christ for the first time or returning to Christ after living away from Him for a number of years. Before we were married, my wife led mission teams to Honduras to plant trees after the horrific Hurricane Mitch destroyed the ecosystem. Through these teams, both participants and locals who volunteered came to faith in Jesus Christ. It is through serving that you—and others—are transformed.

Share how Christ has changed you. The greatest thing you can share is your life. People don't want to be preached at, they want a friend. They want to hear stories and the greatest story you can tell is your own story. They want to hear how Christ has come alive in your heart and how He has become a friend to you.

Realize that it is the working of the Holy Spirit—not what you say or don't say—that points people to Jesus. Jesus said, "The wind blows wherever it pleases. You hear its sound, but you cannot tell where it comes from or where it is going. So it is with everyone born of the Spirit."[13] The work of the Holy Spirit is a mystery. We must remain dependent on Him in sharing our faith and always rely on this truth: engaging people's hearts in spiritual matters and bringing them to Christ is the *Holy Spirit's* work, not ours.

One year while ministering in India, we were up in a small village near Darjeeling (where the tea is made), and I was to speak in a church that met in a small home in the Himalayan mountains. At the last moment, my friend from India was called away to speak at another church—

he was my interpreter! Here I was without an interpreter and I was supposed to preach in one hour. I did not know what I was going to do.

A woman approached me and asked if I needed an interpreter and, of course, you know what I said. "YES! Please, will you interpret for me?"

She agreed and we began to get to know each other. The first thing she told me was she did not believe in Jesus Christ. At first I thought, "She can't possibly interpret for me," but then I began to sense that perhaps God sent her and allowed our paths to cross for some reason. I asked her to please translate what I said word for word. She agreed. We prayed before the service— actually, I prayed. And we were off.

After the three-hour service, my interpreter came up to me and said she wanted to talk. She began telling me she had been considering the claims of Christ for a few months, but did not really know what Christ had to say because she did not have a Bible and no church body in her small village had one. So for the first time, she actually heard the claims of Christ by interpreting my message.

After hearing the message that morning, she said she wanted to follow Christ as the one true God instead of following the millions of Hindu gods. I could not believe it! Had this ever happened before? Had someone ever preached and then became a believer afterwards?

What a happy time! You never know where people have been prior to the moment they hear the Gospel. You never know how the Spirit of God is working, convicting and moving in their hearts. We cannot predict when or how a person will put their faith in Christ. All we can do is remain humble, keep seeking and be faithful in sharing the hope we have as followers of Jesus. As Philemon 6 says, "Be active in sharing your faith, so you will have a full understanding of every good thing we have in Christ."

Questions for Personal Reflection or Small Group Study:

1. If you are in a group, share briefly how you came to Christ. What was the most important factor that led you to Christ? Can you see a similar theme or similarity from each person's story?

2. Think of a time when you experienced someone sharing Christ in a positive and healthy way. What caused you to believe it was done in a healthy way?

3. Have you experienced someone sharing Christ that was done in a damaging way? What caused you to believe it was damaging?

4. When it comes to faith sharing, why is loving people from the heart more important than "knowing the right information"?

Notes

1. John 10:27
2. Romans 10:14-15
3. 1 Timothy 4:12-13
4. 1 Corinthians 1:27
5. John 3:5-6
6. John 3:5-8
7. Ephesians 2:8-10
8. Romans 5:8
9. John 14:6
10. Matthew 7:13-14
11. Philippians 2:12-13
12. Lesslie Newbigin, *The Gospel in a Pluralistic Society* (Eerdmans Publishing, Grand Rapids, Michigan, 1989), 18
13. John 3:7-8

CHAPTER

3

I Want To Bring Them Also

"I have other sheep that are not of this sheep pen. I must bring them also. They too will listen to my voice, and there shall be one flock and one shepherd."—Jesus Christ

"The purpose of Theology is to change the world for the better."—Dietrich Bonhoeffer

"We must win rulers; political, economic, scientific, artistic personalities. They are the engineers of souls. They mold the souls of men. Winning them, you win the people they lead and influence." —Richard Wurmbrand

One year while I was in India, we had a long train ride ahead of us. We were off to visit a new mission site where there were no churches in existence. It was "virgin" territory as far as the Gospel was concerned. We were all excited.

You have never had a real train experience unless you have ridden a train in India. People bring their chickens and goats on the train with them. The smells and noises you hear on the train are unlike anything you have encountered in your life. At night you had better chain your suitcase to your seat or it will surely be gone by morning. Even going to the bathroom is an amazing experience. The bathroom is essentially a small compartment with a hole in the floor that opens to the train tracks below. That's right, when you "gotta go," it goes right out onto the train tracks!

The ride we thought was going to take 20 hours ended up taking over 40. You'll do just about anything to pass the time. I explored the train, counted goats and spent hours staring at the beautiful Indian terrain. At one point on the ride, I began to play my guitar and my friends and I began singing together. The whole train cart gathered close to hear the young Americans sing. After a while, I noticed one man who was sitting there listening and I wanted to ask him a question. I asked through an interpreter, "Do you know who we are singing about?" He said no. I then told him we had just sung a song about Jesus Christ. He replied, "Who is he? A singer from America?"

I could not believe it. As I have told that story in churches and at conferences over the past few years, I am repeatedly surprised by the laughter that comes from the crowd when they hear it. I often ponder why the crowd is laughing. Some crowds laugh louder than others when they hear the story. I believe those who laugh less really understand the power in the story and the heaviness it brings to my heart. How could this man not know who Jesus Christ is? Why would his only connection to the name of Jesus be through a happenstance encounter with a group of Americans on a train?

While I was a college student, I was thrilled with the opportunity to return to the same place in Africa I had visited a few years earlier, Malawi. To be able to return to a distant part of the world and visit old friends from another culture was a blessing I could not get out of my mind. The idea of traveling to another part of the world and *never* developing long-term relationships seemed so futile to me. Perhaps I would meet the chief of that village again or meet the elephant that ate my camera out of the van when I was there a few years earlier.

Upon my arrival, an African pastor told me that we were going the next day to meet the chief of the village where I had shared the Gospel (see Chapter 2). I could not believe it—a reunion! We sat under a tree and the chief finally came and we visited together for several minutes. He then asked me to come to his house for a meal after the church service. I got to preach at the same church where I had preached my first sermon at age 16. The church now had a brick building and many came up to me very thankful I had come back to their village. The pastor asked people to raise their hands if they remembered me coming four years earlier. So many raised their hands I could not believe it!

After church was over, we walked for about 20 minutes through the tall grass to the chief's house. I told my traveling companions we should eat with our hands because that is the way everyone eats in the villages in Africa. I wanted my friends to know how much of a "cultural expert" I was and that I knew how to do things the African way. I was sure they would all be so impressed. As we sat down, we began to eat with our hands and then looked down on the ground to find all the children eating with spoons! They were looking up at us strangely, no doubt wondering why these *goozungus* (white men) were eating with their hands. Needless to say, I felt a little foolish, and we all got a good laugh out of it.

We were in the middle of nowhere and there was no electricity. It seems we were 100 miles past the Great Commission. (If you don't get that joke, don't worry about it.) I remember thinking, *I could not be further from civilization than I am right now.* But then the most amazing thing happened. Our hosts brought each of us a bottle of Coke. I was shocked even further to discover it was cold! Ice cold! I thought, *How could I be in the middle of a village in southeast Africa and be drinking a cold American beverage?*

If you have traveled about the world you know Coca Cola products are available just about anywhere you go. Whether you are in the desserts of the Middle East, the jungles of Africa or the villages of India, Coke is there with you. If you go to the Coca Cola museum in Atlanta, Georgia, you will be amazed at the way their product has managed to infiltrate the entire globe. Their product is known and recognized by almost everyone on the planet.

Why then, I wonder, has it been 2,000 years since Jesus Christ came, and the Gospel has yet to be heard in many parts of the world because there is no Christian church present?

A pastor in Pakistan once told me that every demon in hell has to memorize one verse. It is Matthew 24:14: "The gospel of the Kingdom must be preached to every nation and then the end shall come." The pastor said this verse is written on every demon's bed. They have to read it every night. And before they come to the earth to tempt and to try to destroy Christians, they have to recite the verse to Satan himself.

The devil and his demons know that if the Gospel goes to every nation (the Greek word is *ethane*), then the end will come. The reality is that the devil is a roaring lion seeking whom he may devour. When the Gospel is preached, the orphan and widow are cared for, the oppressed are empowered and the church is about what we are called to be about. When that happens, the chambers of hell shudder in fear. The demonic forces recoil when the people of God are fueled with passion for God's glory. They dread the day when the Gospel is shared with all people on the earth.

Please hear me clearly: I am not suggesting we focus our energy on knowing or trying to manipulate the return of Christ...because we cannot. There are some in the mission community who use this idea as a motivation for missions, but I think one should use caution in doing this. Much of the church spends much energy and time focused on eschatology, the study of the End Times. Just look at the *Left Behind* series and its popularity among Christians!

However, I believe this hyper-focus on End Times doctrine produces in some a passivity and laziness when it comes to moving out in mission to the world. When our attention is captured by looking for "signs of the end," we run the risk of not seeing and responding to the needs of the poor, the lost and the dying around us right now. When someone asks me what my "eschatology" is, which is a good way to get Christians into an argument, I always say, "I only have a missiological eschatology." What I mean is that everything in our Christian theology should be mission oriented. Our study and worship of God should always connect with the ministry of the church to the world. I do think we should long for the coming of Jesus because the Bible says there will be a crown in Heaven for those who do.[1] But we should not spend all of our time and energy discussing and debating it. There is simply too much work to do.

It is reported that Martin Luther was once asked what he would do if Jesus were to return tomorrow. He responded, "I would plant a tree!" We should have that long-term perspective as well.[2]

Many of Jesus' teachings focus on His heart for those who are not in relationship with the Father. Indeed, this is a central theme in many of His parables. But perhaps the clearest proclamation He ever made regarding the motivation of His heart is recorded in Luke 19:10, where He said, "For the Son of Man came to seek and to save what was lost."

Have you ever traveled somewhere in the world and been completely lost? I have many times. I have been lost in countries where I could not find one person who spoke English or one sign written in my native tongue. It has happened to me in places like Baghdad, Iraq; Dhaka, Bangladesh; and countless villages throughout India. It is a helpless and hopeless reality to be trapped in. In a similar way, everyone in the world is born helpless and lost and in need of Jesus Christ. This is our reality—plain and simple.

Jesus is always concerned and wanting people to turn to Him, even those we may have given up on. Jesus said, "I am the good shepherd; I know my sheep and my sheep know me—just as the Father knows me and I know the Father—and I lay down my life for the sheep. I have other sheep that are not of this sheep pen. I must bring them also."[3]

The outcasts of society are often ignored by the church, no matter which culture you look at in the world. This group includes, but is not limited to, orphans, drug abusers, victims of violence, the poor, people with HIV/AIDS, migrant workers, adults and children trafficked into sexual and other forms of slavery, the illiterate, the displaced and those who are deprived of national identity. These are the kind of people who, in my opinion, Jesus would identify with today if He were alive in the flesh. He would not identify with popular church growth specialists, political leaders, or famous mega church pastors—but, rather, with the forgotten.

Remember Jesus' teaching, "When you give a luncheon or dinner, do not invite your friends, your brothers or relatives, or your rich neighbors; if you do, they may invite you back and so you will be repaid. But when you give a banquet, invite the poor, the crippled, the lame, the blind, and you will be blessed. Although they cannot repay you, you will be repaid at the resurrection of the righteous."[4]

Within church culture, you will often hear people express interest in the numbers of people attending a particular church. "How many go to that church?" they ask. I believe Jesus is not merely counting those who are in the church. He is counting those who are not. I always try to remember this as I travel throughout the world and ask that God will continue to break my heart for the lost, the hurting and the destitute. Remember the words of Jesus to His disciples, "Do you not say, 'Four months more and then the harvest'? I tell you, open your eyes and look at the fields! They are ripe for harvest."[5]

Still Over 1 Billion with Very Little Access

Some are aware and others are not. In the world today, over 1 billion live in regions where they cannot hear about Jesus Christ, whether through a local church or a friend. "Why can't they hear about Christ?" you ask. Because there are no Christians there to tell them. Yes, God is able to reveal Himself through dreams and visions, as He did to Saul on the road to Damascus, but most often God desires to use people to convey His love and grace to others.

If you travel to a small town like Brownwood, Texas, you will most likely not meet a Buddhist. Do you think the people in that community regularly hear about Buddhism? Yes, perhaps they see Richard Gere on television, talking about his Buddhist beliefs, or they might read a story in the paper about the Dali Lama's fight for his own people of Tibet. But in all probability very few individuals in this community will ever engage in spiritual discussions regarding the teachings of Buddhism. A similar reality exists for thousands of villages, towns and cities around the world where church communities are not present. I am not writing this because I read it in some book, but because I have been to many places in the world where this is indeed true. In northern countries throughout Africa, throughout the Middle East, across India and China, and in other pockets in Asia, the church is conspicuously absent. I have seen it with my own eyes. People do not have a Christian friend in a village simply because there are no Christians present. Even in a city of 300,000, there may be only a handful of families who name Jesus Christ as Lord. We must let this stark reality awaken within us a compassion that leads us to action

As I've said before, the most effective means of evangelism is relationship. If you don't believe me, try this exercise with your friends, small group or church. Ask people to raise their hands in response to these questions, "Who came to Christ through watching a Christian television program? Who came to Christ by reading a Gospel tract? Who came to Christ through going to a large crusade? Who came to Christ because of a relationship with either a friend or family member who loved you and shared with you about Christ?"

There may a few who come to Christ through the first several ways, but usually the majority raise their hand on the last question. It proves that relationships are the most powerful means of transformation and impacting people.

How will people who do not know Christ come to know Him if there are no Christians around? The answer is, it will be very difficult. We must let this stark reality awaken within us a compassion that leads to action. As Paul wrote, "How then, can they call on the one they have not believed in? And how can they believe in the one of whom they have not heard? And how can they hear without someone preaching to them? And how can they preach unless they are sent? As it is written, 'How beautiful are the feet of those who bring good news!'"[6]

We live in communities in America where it seems there is a church on every corner. In many parts of the country, this is literally true. Too often we define "pioneer" ministry as simply re-telling the Gospel in ways that are relatable and relevant to those in America who already have some understanding of Christ (though it may be inaccurate), and who have had some experience of church (though it may not have been relevant or meaningful). While this is healthy and needed, we must not neglect those regions of the world where the church of Jesus Christ is still very fragile or may not even exist. This is true "pioneer" ministry. We must encourage the church to always think globally about God's redemptive plan for the world.

Many churches in America are already reaching out to these unchurched regions, but so much more needs to be done. Of course, for the reality of the world's great need to impact us on a heart level, we need the work of the Holy Spirit and not merely my own meager attempt to convince you. I pray that the Holy Spirit will convict us all, and that God's kindness will lead us to repentance and a concern for the millions who do not know him.[7]

One year I spent the entire summer in East Indonesia, in a place called Irian Jaya. Only a few decades ago the people of this region were cannibals and had little influence from other cultures. All summer long we worked in constructing a wall around a training center for Pastors.

We lived with the students and shared meals with them. I will never forget when our team said farewell to the new friends we had met during our time there. They literally wept for hours on our shoulders because we were leaving. I will forever be moved by the sorrow they expressed over the likelihood that we would never see each other again until we get to heaven.

There is a need for us as followers of Jesus to be filled with grief and sorrow over the millions of people on our planet who are separated from God and who need to enter into a relationship with Him through Jesus Christ. The Bible says, "As he approached Jerusalem and saw the city, he wept over it."[8] The meaning of the word "wept" here is not a silent cry. The Greek word is *klaio* (klah'-yo). It means to sob and wail aloud. This is what Jesus did as He looked over Jerusalem.

I like what Matthew Henry says about this moment in Jesus' life: "The great Ambassador from heaven is here making his public entry into Jerusalem, not to be respected there, but to be rejected; he knew what a nest of vipers he was throwing himself into."[9]

Jesus cares deeply for the lost—even though He knows many of them will reject Him. His tenacious love for the world reverberates through most of His teachings. But perhaps it is most clearly expressed through His parables of lost sheep and a lost coin:

> *Suppose one of you has a hundred sheep and loses one of them. Does he not leave the ninety-nine in the open country and go after the lost sheep until he finds it? And when he finds it, he joyfully puts it on his shoulders and goes home. Then he calls his friends and neighbors together*

and says, "Rejoice with me; I have found my lost sheep." I tell you that in the same way there will be more rejoicing in heaven over one sinner who repents than over ninety-nine righteous persons who do not need to repent.

Or suppose a woman has ten silver coins and loses one. Does she not light a lamp, sweep the house and search carefully until she finds it? And when she finds it, she calls her friends and neighbors together and says, "Rejoice with me; I have found my lost coin." In the same way, I tell you, there is rejoicing in the presence of the angels of God over one sinner who repents.[10]

At the very heart of God is His love for all the world and His desire for humanity to know Him and to worship Him. The Bible says God has poured out His love for us in that while we were still sinners, Christ died for us.[11] Jesus modeled this love through both His life and His teaching. He is tenaciously seeking the lost and the outcast—people who some would never consider "good candidates" for Christianity. The Bible says, "The Lord is not slow in keeping his promise, as some understand slowness. He is patient with you, not wanting anyone to perish, but everyone to come to repentance."[12]

There are literally billions of people in the world today who do not confess with their mouths that Jesus is Lord and who do not believe He was raised from the dead.[13] They search for meaning through endless ritual, trying to find hope by performing certain acts of religious duty. But all the while, they feel spiritually bankrupt, empty and bruised. As followers of Jesus we must allow ourselves to be moved from sorrow to action as our Lord was by the lostness of humanity.

A Woman in India Sacrifices Her Own Baby

Going to Varanassi, India for the first time was an overwhelming experience. Varanasi is the Mecca of Hinduism—meaning that it is the holiest city in the Hindu religion. There are more than 25,000 Hindu temples there, and the holy river, the Ganges, runs through the city. Hindus believe that if you bathe in this holy river your sins will be removed and you will break the cycle of reincarnation. Hindus also believe that if after you die you are cremated in Varanassi, you will break the cycle of reincarnation. It is a holy city, yet filled with much hopelessness. You see it in people's eyes.

One day while I was in this city, I was sitting with an Indian pastor and we were praying for people to come to know Christ and for the church in the area. After some time in prayer, the Indian pastor told me a story that will haunt me for as long as I live. A young girl, probably only 18 years of age, came to the Ganges River in Varanassi with her only child. She walked to the Ganges weighed down with guilt and shame over her sins, and believed she had to sacrifice her only child to the gods in order for her sins to be removed. She lifted her own baby in the air and said some mantras (Hindu prayers) then threw her baby in the river. A local Indian evangelist was watching this happen from a distance and could not believe what he was seeing. *This woman must be on drugs or has gone crazy,* the evangelist thought. He ran down to her and asked, "What is wrong? What have you done?"

The young, poor Hindu girl replied, "The sins on my heart are too many so I had to offer the best I have to the gods in order for my sins to be removed... I offered my own child."

"You did not have to do that!" exclaimed the evangelist. "Your sins have been paid for in the death of Jesus Christ. His blood has been shed and we can receive forgiveness of all our sin. Our hearts can be washed white as snow."

The girl looked despondent, saying, "Why could you not have come five minutes earlier to tell me this amazing news? Then I would not have had to throw my child into the river?"

Can the Blood of a Goat Bring Life?

The line was too long to even see the end. The people in Calcutta, India, were standing with their chests touching the back of the person in front of them. Hundreds of people, perhaps thousands, were waiting to enter the Kali temple. Kali is the Hindu goddess of destruction. Every one of the people in line was holding a small rope attached to a goat. They were taking the goat to the temple to sacrifice it to Kali. I was able to witness this spectacle firsthand—blood flooding down the sidewalk like water after a rainstorm, the piercing sounds of goats squealing, and people leaving the temple with blood from the goat applied to their heads and clothes. Whatever Hindu teaching prompted this act, the result was these people believed that the blood of the goat offered power—perhaps power to forgive their sin, heal their sickness or bless their family.

This is similar, of course, to Hebrew rituals that have gone on for thousands of years. But as the Bible says, "...those sacrifices are an annual reminder of sins because it is impossible for the blood of bulls and goats to take away sins... we have been made holy through the sacrifice of the body of Jesus Christ once for all."[14]

Lights Shine Brightest in Darkness

We got our visas to Baghdad after waiting three days in Amman, Jordan. We had to get our visas put on a separate sheet of paper instead of on our passports. Finally, we were on our way. It was 1996 and Saddam Hussein was still in power. The drive from Amman took more than 14 hours. As we drove into Baghdad I began to see that this once self-sufficient and rich nation was not in good condition. The heat was unlike anything I had ever experienced. It was well over 120 degrees Fahrenheit.

As we drove around in the city with the windows rolled down, the wind hitting your face felt like a blast from a furnace, I saw buildings in decay, children begging on the streets, and a level of poverty far more severe than I had expected. We went to a local hotel, but were denied admittance and told we had to stay at the El-Rashid Hotel. The El-Rashid is a five-star hotel without the five-star prices. We got our room for a mere $20 per night. We were later told that our rooms were bugged by Iraqi officials.

During the week, I was invited to preach at a women's meeting. On the drive to the church, my taxi driver got lost and started driving around in circles, and I wondered what the secret police were thinking as they were following in the car behind me. I finally arrived at the church and was moved to see the Iraqi believers worshiping God. I preached on how God has used women throughout history to proclaim Christ to the world. I spoke on how a woman, Mary Magdalene, was the first person to testify on the resurrection of Jesus.[15]

After the service I was brought to another room where we discussed issues with some of the believers who spoke English. After a short while, I was told that an officer from the government had arrived to question me. We went to another room where I was told he was from the government's office of religious affairs. He asked me many questions and I quickly realized he was suspicious of my motives. He asked, "Why did you want to come to Iraq when your country does not want you to?"

I answered, "I love the people of Iraq because God loves the people of Iraq." After we spoke for nearly an hour, he was happy to know Americans cared for the people of Iraq. He told me he would help me in the future if I needed help. I told him I would like to come back to Iraq and I would need help in getting visas.

He replied, "No problem, I will give you and anyone you want visas to come to Iraq. You are most welcome." It was encouraging to see such bright lights in Iraq among the followers of Jesus. Although they were few in number, they shined bright as beacons of hope. Despite international sanctions and persecution in Iraq after the Gulf War, the church was alive. It was a joy to be with them.

Be a Big Light

If you grew up as a child in the church you probably sang a song that went, "This little light of mine, I'm gonna let it shine... Hide it under a bushel, NO... I'm gonna let it shine... let it shine, let it shine, let it shine."

I sang this little song growing up and frankly never liked it. I always thought, *I don't want to be a little light but a big light.* I didn't want to be told I'm a little light, but that I could do great things for God and could shine as bright as God would allow me to shine. I wanted to be like the Luxor light; not a small light.

If you ever go to Las Vegas at night you will no doubt see a bright beam of light shining into the sky. It comes from the Luxor Hotel & Casino. It is the brightest light in the world (or so it is promoted). The average light bulb used to light a room is about 75 watts. The bulb at the Luxor is 350,000 watts. It is said that if you were sitting in a spacecraft 10 miles above the earth, you could read a newspaper by the light of the Luxor. You can see the Luxor light 250 miles away from an airplane flying at 30,000 feet.

Jesus said, "You are the light of the world. A city on a hill cannot be hidden. Neither do people light a lamp and put it under a bowl. Instead they put it on its stand, and it gives light to everyone in the house. In the same way, let your light shine before men, that they may see your good deeds and praise your Father in heaven."[16]

The great missionary from England, William Carey, said, "Attempt Great things for God. Expect Great things from God." He was a man whom God used to shine a bright light into a lost world. You should read about some of the other people God has used in great ways and whose lights shined bright: William Booth, Adoniram Judson, J. Hudson Taylor, Jim Elliott, Amy Carmichael and Corrie Ten Boon.

I fully believe that when the lostness of humanity breaks our hearts and consumes us, we will begin to grasp a portion of God's heart for the world and we will never be the same. We will want our lives, our families, and our churches to be lights that shine brightly in the world. We will spend our money differently and take vacations differently. We will consume less so we can give away more money to world evangelization and alleviating human suffering. We will attempt great things for God and expect great things from God. God is in the business of transformation. Let us pray that He will transform us as His people to become like Christ.

Engaging Someone from another Religion

I believe it is a very good idea to study other faiths and to know how to engage in a conversation with someone from another religion. But when you talk with someone from another religion, no matter what the religion is, it is important to see past the ritual and even their belief in that ritual or their doctrine, and get to more fundamental issues to discuss with them.

Let's take Hinduism for example. Within Hindu culture there are dozens of festivals. Honestly, it's hard to keep up with them all. And if you ask 10 Hindus about the meaning of one particular festival—say Divali, for example—you will most likely get 10 different answers. Although Divali is a very important festival, maybe the most important, many devout Hindus approach the festival differently and draw different meanings from it. This is not like our experience as Christians. If you ask a bunch of devout Christians about the true meaning of Easter, you will usually get only one response: Easter is a celebration of the resurrection of Jesus Christ.

I was once in Kathmandu, Nepal, during the Divali festival, which is also known as the Festival of Lights. It looks like Christmastime because every shop and house is covered in what we think of as Christmas lights. The lights are said to be able to "get the attention of the gods."

The day before I arrived was the Divali "crow *puja*." The day I attended was the "dog *puja*," and the day after that was the "cow *puja*." *Puja* means "worship." Hindus worship these different animals because they each represent a different Hindu god.

Dogs, for example, represent lord Bhairab. I actually kept the front page of the Kathmandu Post from the day I attended the festival. There is a photo on that page of a bunch of police dogs in training. Their fur was covered with flowers, and *tickas* were applied to their foreheads. The article described how the policemen worship the dog on that day. It was not something you see on the front page of most American newspapers.

I say all this to illustrate how the festivals all take on different meanings for different Hindus, depending on their role in life and what part of the country they are from. A Hindu living in Londo is probably going to have a different interpretation than a Hindu living in a small village regarding what the festival of Divali (or any other festival) is supposed to mean.

This leads to an important principle when discussing faith with a Hindu (or, for that matter, a person from any faith system). When I engage Hindus, I *first* try to listen and learn about the meaning of the festival from their point of view, then I try and draw bridges of similarity between their belief and my own faith in Jesus Christ. For example, I often ask questions such as, "What brings you hope about this certain Hindu god or festival?" or "How does this help you love better and become a better person?" or "How does this allow you to have peace at night for the wrongs you have done?" and so on. All of these questions allow me in turn to share how I have found hope, forgiveness, peace and love in Christ.

By focusing the conversation on our shared values—finding meaning, peace, contentment in life or the ability to love those who wrong me—I can easily share my own story or a story from the Bible in a non-offensive way. All the while, of course, I am praying that the Holy Spirit will allow this person to see Jesus and to desire to learn more about Him.

Usually, the Hindus in India and Nepal are happy to talk about these issues, as they typically have never looked beneath their rituals to consider their deeper meaning. In fact, I've found that most people in the world—regardless of their religion—love to talk about the deeper issues of meaning, purpose and identity. So when engaging people from other faiths, approach them with an attitude of curiosity, asking lots of questions rather than giving a lot of answers. If you do this, you will usually get a chance later in the conversation to share your perspective.

Run to the Pain and Embrace It—Don't Hide!

Without a heart and passion for the lost, Christians tend to fall into a "protect ourselves from them" posture in life. In truth, Christians have always been good at running from danger toward comfort. We start our own schools, build our own business networks, establish our own health clubs, and totally insulate ourselves from those who do not know God. We do it all in the name of "keeping ourselves pure," or "reaching out to our community," but that is not what mostly happens. The sad truth is, we create these facilities mostly for our own comfort. I have never had anyone tell me how they came to Jesus because they saw a church build a $3 million health club.

Why does the church in the West fall into the trap of "keeping up with the Joneses"? The most important fruit that can come out of church facilities are relationships and conversations that lead people to know Christ. But doesn't it make more sense to "go to the lost in their facilities" rather than try to lure them to "come to us in our facilities"?

Of course, I'm not saying the church in the West should never own land or build its own structures. There is sound financial wisdom in owning your own property. I just wonder at times how Jesus would respond if He came to earth in person today and saw churches filled with shops, bowling allies and elaborate water fountains, costing in the hundreds of thousands of dollars.

Consider what's happened over the past few decades in the urban centers of most North America cities. Those districts should be filled with people transformed by the Gospel, not just hollow old church buildings. Churches in those areas have dwindled down to very small congregations as most Christians move to the suburbs. Has our desire for the American Dream kept us from living the life that Jesus called us to live?

For many in the West the answer is yes. Why has the church not run to the roughest neighborhoods and highest crime areas to be the presence of Christ there and to impact those areas for positive change? Have we prioritized our own safety and growing our church budget at the expense of living a life of mission and going to where the poor and hurting are?

Thankfully, many followers of Jesus are not satisfied with this "retreat mentality" and are moving back to the city centers. The crime rate may be a little higher and the schools may not be as good as the suburbs, but they are there to fulfill God's mission and to be a conduit of God's love to the lost. They are putting their kids into "public" schools and teaching them to be missionaries there.

Many others are going to the countries of the world labeled "unsafe" by the State Department, but that are filled with people in need of God's love. They are not letting anything stop them from finding a way to get there, even if it means selling their own possessions. These folks are on mission with God's mission, which is to redeem all creation and people to Himself. I hope you are one of them.

I know some of you are asking yourself, "Are you trying to say that everyone should move to the inner city or a foreign country in order to follow God?" or "Do you realize how rich you have to be to live in any urban center in North America?" Well my short answer is no, not everyone has to pick up and move in order to be faithful to God. But if you are bored and not stretched in your life and walk with God, then I encourage you to move somewhere that will stretch you and challenge you. That could mean across your city or across the ocean. You can find a job in any city in the world teaching English or any number of other needed skills. And all urban centers in America have affordable areas to live. It might not be in the area you prefer, but it will be among those you most need to help.

As Christ followers we cannot live by and be conformed to the systems of the world—which are greed, materialism, lust, pride and self-centeredness, to name a few. As the Bible says, "But just as he who called you is holy, so be holy in all you do; for it is written: 'Be holy, because I am holy.'"[17] We need wisdom and counsel on how to not be conformed to this world, but how to be transformed by the renewing of our minds as Paul wrote in Romans 12:1-2.

At the same time, we cannot constantly point our fingers at our culture and say the problem is only with them "out there." Many Christians expressed grave concern when prayer was taken out of schools, but I think God is more concerned when Christians have stopped praying. In a similar way, some Christians accused our society of losing moral clarity when the Ten Commandments were taken out of public areas. I assert that it is more of a problem when the followers of Jesus stop living and obeying them. My point is simple. As Eugene Peterson paraphrases, "Don't point out the toothpick in someone else's eye when you have a telephone poll in your own eye." The tendency for Christians to isolate, point their fingers, and judge is something we must be careful to avoid.

Instead, look at the culture around you like the missionary Christ has called you to be, and constantly pray for ways to connect and relate to those around you. Perhaps it will be through music, photography, children, travel, sports, hiking or art. Whatever it is, begin to simply see that people are people—no less and no more—no matter how they dress, talk, look or smell. They are simply people who need to hear, to experience and to know about the love of God. God is more concerned with the journey and not just the destination we are so often consumed with. The journey of faith is focused on knowing God, and it begins when we come to Christ; it's not merely about going to heaven when we die. This journey should be filled with bringing as many as possible with us to know God, too.

Of course, while we should be captivated by the lostness of the world, we cannot immerse ourselves in the world to the point that we lose our distinctiveness and integrity as followers of Jesus. Neither can we allow ourselves to become isolated from the culture in which we live. It is not an easy balance and there is great tension in this issue, but we must remember the heart of the great evangelist himself, Paul, who wrote, "I make myself a slave to everyone, to win as many as possible. To the Jews I became like a Jew, to win the Jews. To those under the law I became like one under the law (though I myself am not under the law), so as to win those under the law. To those not having the law I became like one not having the law (though I am not free from God's law but am under Christ's law), so as to win those not having the law. To the weak I became weak, to win the weak. I have become all things to all men so that by all possible means I might save some. I do all this for the sake of the gospel, that I may share in its blessings."[18]

I encourage you to meditate on Psalms 23, not written as most know it, but paraphrased from the perspective of one who does not know God. This is how millions of people in the world think, feel and live their lives without knowing God through Jesus Christ:

I have no shepherd.
I want and am in need.
I have no one to feed me in green pastures,
I have no rest.
I have no one to lead me to quiet waters.
I am thirsty.
I have no one to guide me in the right ways.
I don't know where to turn.
As I walk through the valley of the shadow of death,
evil surrounds me;
I am terribly afraid for no one is with me to comfort
me.
I have no feast prepared for me.
I am overwhelmed by my enemies.
No one anoints my wounds or fills my cup.
My cup is empty.
All the days of my life are filled with disappointment
and deceit.
I have no home for eternity.
Will I dwell in an evil house forever?[19]

Questions for Personal Reflection or Small Group Study:

1. How do you make an intentional effort to get to know someone who does not know God?

2. What could you do to meet more people who do not know God or who are curious about the things of God?

3. Who do you know from another religion? How might you effectively engage with this person to discuss their faith?

4. What are some ways you have isolated yourself from the lost world around you? How could you begin to re-engage the world in a healthy way?

5. How can you practically help lost people in other cultures around the world come to know God?

Notes

1. see 2 Timothy 4:8
2. James F.Engel and William A. Dyrness, *Changing the Mind of World Missions: Where Have We Gone Wrong?* (Intervarsity Press, Downers Grove, IL, 2000), 160
3. John 10:14-16
4. **Luke 14:12-14**
5. John 4:35-36
6. Romans 10:14-15
7. see Romans 2:4
8. Luke 19:41
9. Matthew Henry, *Matthew Henry's Commentary on the Whole Bible: New Modern Edition*, electronic database (Hendrickson Publishers, Inc., 1991)
10. Luke 15:3-10
11. see Romans 5:8
12. 2 Peter 3:9
13. see Romans 10:9
14. Hebrews 10:3-4, 10
15. John 20:18
16. Matthew 5:14-16
17. 1 Peter 1:15-16
18. 1 Corinthians 9:19-23
19. author unknown

CHAPTER
4

Living Simply So Others May Simply Live

"The love of worldly possessions is a sort of birdlime, which entangles the soul and prevents it flying to God."
—Augustine of Hippo

"Riches are the instrument of all vices, because they render us capable of putting even our worst desires into execution."—Ambrose

"There are three conversions necessary: the conversion of the heart, mind, and the purse."—Martin Luther

One year I was back in the Sudanese refugee camps in Uganda. I was meeting with several dozen pastors and interviewing them and seeing ways we could serve and support their churches and ministries. The day before we were to meet them, four young men came to our little hotel. They knew the one Sudanese pastor who was with us. I found out they were all young evangelists and were about to return to Sudan for their ministry. They spoke of their home villages and how many of their family members and friends had been killed through the civil war over the many years. I sat with these four young men and asked them if they would like a Coke or Sprite to drink. They all began to look at each other with surprise and one of them, John, raised his eyebrows in excitement. I later learned they had never had a Coke.

The next day these four guys came to our meeting. As I began to talk to John, I learned his story through an interpreter. John was merely 20 years old. He got married at 17 and could not pay his dowry, a mere $40. He was a refugee and had no job. Forty dollars could have very well been a million. After being married for one year, John's wife conceived and gave birth to their son. However, during her pregnancy and labor, John was not allowed to be with her. In fact, he had never been able to see his own child since the birth. His son was a year-and-half-old.

In Africa culture, the male pays the dowry to the woman's family. This dowry could be in the form of a cow, a few chickens or money. For John, the money was demanded and because he could not pay it, he could not take his bride from her parents' home.

As I talked to John, I could hear the pain in his voice, his love for his family and his desire to be united with them. I realized I should help him. I told him later in the day that I represented Christians from America who are concerned and who care about the body of Christ in Africa, specifically Sudan. I told him we wanted him to be united with his family so he could return to Sudan and start his own church. I gave the money to the local leader to make sure the payment of the dowry would be carried out.

What happened next is something I will never forget. John got on the ground and kissed my feet in gratitude. He realized his dowry would be paid and he could be united with his wife and see his son for the first time.

A few years later, I was back in the refugee camps teaching at a pastor's conference. As I arrived in the building, a dark man came running to me with a big smile. We threw our arms around each other and embraced; he told me he had heard of my coming and walked several days from Sudan to see me. His son was doing great and John and his wife had a second child.

I will never forget what a mere $40 can do.

I grew up around wealth in suburban America. Even as a young boy some of my friends' families had private jets and second and third homes. I remember in grade school flying with one of my friends on his family's private jet to go skiing for the weekend in Colorado. Just for the weekend! *This is normal*, I thought. *I am sure most kids get to do this kind of thing.* I soon realized that most do not. Although I saw images and heard people tell stories of how people suffered around the world, I was mostly blinded from poverty.

I thought everyone was alright and got by fine. I was sucked into a consumer culture that said, "Buy more and consume more and you will be happy." Really, everyone living in North America gets caught up in the consumer mindset to one degree or another, and it is hard to break the power of this lie.

Another lie I learned quickly was, "Possessions are good to accumulate. Toys are a necessity, both for children and adults." As I grew up I slowly began to see the saddening truth. These "lessons" about consumption and possessions are actually a reflection of America's greatest values today. We have become a nation obsessed with consuming and possessing—not freedom and justice for all. I heard one time that the money spent on storage garages in North America exceeds the GNP of many countries in the world. Wow! Our excess belongings that don't even fit into our homes are valued greater than the entire economies of some countries' education, health and basic development needs.

Slaves to Riches?

Many people are simply slaves to riches. Many of us think one has to have wealth and, therefore, we have become slaves to it. But the simple fact is you don't have to be rich to be a slave to riches. The poor can be a slave to wealth just as much as the rich. The core of the matter is not the size of our portfolio, our ability to retire by age 45, or how poor we are. The real issue is: Are our hearts and motives pure? Are we devoted to Jesus first and concerned with His purposes around the world? Is our commitment to invest in the Kingdom of God greater than our commitment to our own financial security and wealth?

Jesus calls us to be a slave to himself.[1] The entire goal of spiritual formation is for our obedience and loyalty to rest in Jesus and in His purposes on earth, just as He taught in the Scriptures. It has become too easy for us to forget the abundance we have in our country while billions live without the basic necessities of life.

When I was in Egypt, I met a man with an arm that was crooked. When I asked what had happened, he explained he had broken it at a young age and because he had no access to medical care it was never set properly. Mahatmas Gandhi said, "The world has enough for every man's need, but not enough for every man's greed." Now the need Gandhi was referring to was not the need for a vacation in the Caymans or U2's latest album, but the basic needs of survival for any human being: food, water, shelter and basic medical care.

I have traveled in more than 70 nations and have seen human suffering in some of the poorest regions on our globe. It is always interesting to hear people's opinions of poverty when they see it first hand. I have heard comments like, "Jesus said we will always have the poor with us, so why do anything?" or "Why do people suffer like this when there is so much wealth in the world?" or "The poor are so much closer to God."

The fact is poverty is often over-spiritualized. Some may believe the poor walk through life closer to God or love God more than people who are not poor. Indeed, you can find Scripture to support this position. Look at the story of the rich man and Lazarus. James wrote, "Has not God chosen those who are poor in the eyes of the world to be rich in faith and to inherit the kingdom he promised those who love him?"[2]

On the other hand, while looking at the Scriptures, you cannot ignore the material wealth of people who loved God: Abraham, Moses, Job, King Solomon and Zacchaeus, to name a few. Jesus did not say it was hard for the poor to enter the Kingdom of God, He did say it was difficult for the rich. In Luke's account of the Sermon on the Mount, Jesus begins by saying, "Blessed are the poor."

Historically, the poor in many countries respond to the Gospel in far greater numbers than the rich do. You need look no further than Africa or the low caste within India to see an abundance of examples.

Surely this issue of whether it's better to be poor or rich in God's eyes will always be debated within the church. But the real issue isn't about the level of wealth we have or don't have. It's about the condition of our hearts when it comes to money. To that end, allow me to suggest a few thoughts on a believer's relationship with money.

• **Money is an Issue of Discipleship**. In our process of spiritual formation—becoming like Christ in our thoughts and behavior—we must always see our relationship with money as a key indicator of our growth and maturity. Particularly to Americans, the definition of "success" has become tightly intertwined with obtaining more wealth and possessions. But that definition falls woefully short of the Bible's ideals. As Christ's disciples, we must master money for the sake of the Kingdom of God and not let money master us. Jesus talked more about money in his teachings than any other subject aside from the Kingdom of God. And the emphasis of those teachings was never about getting rich. In fact, more often than not, it was about giving riches away.

I believe that in our own journeys we should seek relationships with the poor and the oppressed both in our own communities and around the world. Jesus said what you have done to the least of these (the poor) by feeding, clothing and loving them, you have done unto him.[3] Perhaps one reason Jesus so strongly emphasized ministry to the poor is because he knew we would meet and experience *Him* in the midst of loving and serving the poor.

• **Our Standard of Living Should Reflect Christ's Desire for the World, not Our Culture's Desire to Consume.** Many good Christians in North America have added an 11th commandment to their belief system: "With every increase in my salary, my standard of living must also increase." Surely, the materialism that is within the church in the U.S. is appalling to God. Why is it we feel we have to buy things we don't need with money we don't have to impress people we don't know? We consume too much and collect piles of excess stuff that does nothing for us but clog up our lives—from our video games and our televisions, right down to our designer clothes and

$200 shoes. There is an estimated $850 billion per year of disposable income among evangelicals in the United States.[4] We radically need instruction and change in this area. Imagine how many resources could be unleashed for Kingdom work if Christians radically reduced their luxuries?

• **Money is an Issue of Global Missions and Justice.** Our goal as Christ followers is not just for our own personal spiritual healing and growth. We are involved in the expansion and growth of the Kingdom of God in the world. Jesus has clearly told us to make disciples of all nations as we live our lives and travel.[5] We are to be like salt and light in tasteless and dark cultures around the globe. We are a part of a worldwide movement of God in the world. This is no choice but an invitation by God himself. Think of the excitement you have when someone sends you an invitation to a party or wedding. You feel honored and loved. God himself has invited us to join him in reconciling the world and all nations to himself. There still exist over 1,800 distinct ethnic groups in the world without a church in their culture. We are to champion and speak for justice, human rights, the environment and peace in the world.

One of the hats I wear is that of a fund raiser. I love asking people for money. I am not asking them for money for myself or to invest in a business venture to make them more money. I am asking them to invest into the Kingdom of God and to further the cause of Christ around the world. There is no greater cause than this. It bothers me how some Christians seem to look down on missionaries who have to raise their own support while at the same time they don't mind giving their money to non-Christian causes. Some denominations hire "professional" missionaries and pay them a salary. If we are going to advance the Gospel among every people group, we must explore and embrace new models of funding missions. Paul was a great fundraiser. When he wanted to go to Spain to preach the Gospel, he boldly asked the church in Rome to help support his ministry to get there.[6]

I often meet people who are fearful of raising money or fear they will be perceived as "beggars for God" or "wanting an easy hand out" in order to be a missionary. This fear—that is so pervasive within the Body of Christ— is from the devil himself. Missionaries, mission organizations, and causes always have more need than funding. What a great problem it would be if missions had more money than they could spend? Is that realistic, you ask? Consider this: 80 percent of the world's evangelical wealth is in North America—and that total alone represents *more than enough* to fund many more workers in the Great Commission.[7]

Debt That Consumes Us

Perhaps the biggest issue for the prevention of sending more missionaries to the field and supporting mission organizations is the financial debt Christians are in. As George Barna points out, 33 percent of U.S. born-again Christians say it is impossible for them to get ahead in life because of the financial debt they have incurred.[8]

If you are consumed with debt and feel God is leading you to go overseas, I challenge you never to give up your dream. If God is calling you, He will make a way. First, you must seek financial counsel. Also, seek counsel from your pastor and from mission leaders you know. Share your story with them, be honest about the financial obstacles you face, and listen to their advice.

Second, you need to become more financially literate. In order to be a faithful steward of the income God provides you, you need to understand how money works and how to make money a servant of God's purposes in your life and in the world—instead of remaining in the trap of being a servant to money (which is really what "being in debt" is). There are several great financial books available to help you become a better steward of your finances. A few are *The Millionaire Next Door* by Thomas J. Stanley, Ph.D. and William D. Danko, Ph.D., and *Rich Dad, Poor Dad* by Robert T. Kiyosaki. To free yourself from debt, these authors advocate destroying all unnecessary credit cards, and finding ways to reduce your monthly expenses so you can pay off your debt more quickly.

If you are a student or recent college graduate who is struggling with debt and wanting to serve overseas, let me share with you some additional advice I learned from veteran missiologist Ralph Winter. He encourages students to distinguish between two forms of debt: consumer debt and student loans. If you have a lot of consumer debt through credit cards then you need to delay going to the mission field until you've paid off the debt in full. You will need to find a way to reduce your monthly expenses, and perhaps get a second or even third job to pay this off. However, if your debt is in the form of student loans, Winter suggests you factor the monthly cost of these loans into your fundraising. Most donors would be pleased to know that you received further training, in whatever field, before going to the mission field; many are willing to support your education efforts.[9] Of course, as I mentioned earlier, I suggest getting professional counsel on this issue before moving forward with any plan, but I agree with this advice.

The important thing to remember is God wants to free you from debt and allow you to be a generous giver of your income to the cause of Christ in the world. If you commit your finances to God, He will lead you to the right way to accomplish this.

It is Better to Give

One of the hardest spiritual disciplines to practice is giving. But giving truly is a vital means of growth and blessing in our discipleship process. "Remembering the words the Lord himself said: 'It is more blessed to give than to receive.'"[10] However, the average donation by adults who attend U.S. Protestant churches is only about $17 a week.[11] That's less than the cost of a pizza and a movie, and no where close to a true tithe (10 percent of income) for most Americans.

Indeed God wants to make us all more generous givers. We cannot out give God. What could happen if there was a generous revolution in giving among Christians of all ages? Imagine how the world would change in a single year if Christians gave a full 10 percent of their income to the advancement of God's Kingdom in the world. Imagine what would happen if those who could gave 15, 20 or even 50 percent or more of their income to the cause of Christ. It is not unreasonable to expect that such a revolution would bring an end to hunger and disease in many nations around the world—and spark a spiritual awakening like never before.

How could such a revolution begin? It could begin with you. Gandhi said, "You must be the change you want to see in the world."

Perhaps God Gifted You to Make Money

One of the misunderstandings some Christians struggle with is the belief that in order for them to "serve the Lord" they have to walk away from what they love and enjoy doing in the business world to go into full time Christian ministry at a church or campus or on the mission field. I have seen countless numbers of people pursue what others defined as "serving the Lord" and in the process forsake their true God-given gifts, talents and abilities in the market place. Let me encourage you to pursue what you are passionate about and enjoy doing. God has created all of us with different skills and abilities. For many, going to the mission field is not what you should do—but perhaps you are able to support 100 others to get there.

A good question to ask is not, "How much money can I potentially make in my career?" but "How much money do I need to provide for my family and basic needs?" Then after determining that and sticking to it, ask, "How much money can I give away to the cause of Christ through my career?" Then your purpose and motivation at work begins to take on a different focus. I have met people who desire to double what they give away to missions every year. What a worthy goal! You work harder to close that deal and grow your business not for that second home you don't really need, but so you can give away more to spreading the hope of the Gospel throughout the world and alleviating human suffering in the name of Jesus Christ.

Getting Overseas Through a Career

Perhaps you have gifts and abilities in a certain vocation and want to use that vocation to make a global impact. "What could I ever do with my accounting degree?" you may ask. The reality is you can do many things to make a strategic impact for Christ among people in the world who need to know the love of God. A career as an accountant, engineer or teacher can open the right door to get you overseas to places where a traditional missionary cannot go. The trend of sending professionals into the world to use their vocation to meet and minister to people is being embraced by many. To learn more, ask your church leaders for information on the many programs or organizations that focus on sending professionals overseas for the cause of Christ.

A Life of Faith

The Bible says, "Now faith is being sure of what we hope for and certain of what we do not see."[12] All of us as Christians are called to a life of faith. The Bible further says, "And without faith it is impossible to please God, because anyone who comes to him must believe that he exists and that he rewards those who earnestly seek him."[13] God is always wanting to build and grow our faith. In fact, one way God may desire for you to grow in faith is to give up one year or two years or your whole career to live and serve overseas among an oppressed and marginalized people group.

You've decided you don't want to settle for the American dream of independence, personal rights, the pursuit of pleasure, safety, freedom and security. You want something more—a life of faith that will call you to perhaps go hungry at times or live without the pleasures others around you have. You don't want to retire one day and then ask yourself, "Is that it? I have lived a comfortable and predictable life, but what have I really accomplished with the time I was given?" In contrast, how wonderful it would be to come to the end of your life and echo the words of the great Apostle Paul, "I know what it is to be in need, and I know what it is to have plenty. I have learned the secret of being content in any and every situation, whether well fed or hungry, whether living in plenty or in want. I can do everything through him who gives me strength."[14]

It is the love and ambition of money that keeps many people away from following God's call to make disciples of all nations and alleviate human suffering in the world. Excuses are made, lifestyle choices are embraced, and financial debt consumes. Perhaps you are reading this and God's Spirit is speaking to you. You may be like the rich young ruler Jesus told to sell all of his possessions and give them to the poor in order to be a disciple of Jesus. It was the young ruler's love of his possesions that kept him from giving his whole life to Jesus and His Kingdom. But what about you? What's keeping you from giving your whole life to Jesus and His Kingdom?

The Bible says the man did not do what Jesus told him to do and walked away a sad man. Don't make the mistake the young ruler did and live a sad life.

I realize I am speaking boldy, so allow me to clarify what I am saying: Living this call to radical obedience is not merely an issue of riches or geography. It is first and foremost an issue of the heart. Even so, I pray this book will, by God's grace, encourage and motivate many to leave the comfort and safety of a predictable life and embark on a journey to serve the poor, the lost, the broken and the oppressed throughout the world.

Start Now!

In closing this chapter, I want to share a few stories from my personal experiences that hopefully will inspire you to begin now to grow in the area of giving and stewardship:

• **A Poor Woman in Houston.** One summer while I was in college, I worked on staff in an inner-city church in Houston, Texas. One Sunday as I was locking up, a Hispanic woman said she had to go get her tithe for that day and asked if I could wait while she went to get it. Little did I know that I would wait for 45 minutes while she walked home. I got impatient and was very hungry.

Finally, she arrived and handed me the small envelope and went on her way. I saw that it was open, so I looked inside and found one dime. That's right, a 45-minute walk for 10 cents. I could not believe it.

• **A Plane ticket to Indonesia.** Many years ago, I needed $3,000 in just three days to be able to spend eight weeks in ministry in Irian Jaya, Indonesia. I was going to be with a team working at a local Bible training school and doing ministry around the island for the summer. I did not think it would happen and began to pray. The next day I went to my home church and people began coming up to me handing me envelopes. There were probably 15 or so people who did this. The amount equaled exactly $3,100.

• **Eight-Year-Old Jessica in Las Vegas.** I got this letter one day in the mail and was moved by the action of a young girl in Las Vegas, Nevada.

> *Dear Joel,*
> *My name is Jessi. About six months ago I read your newsletter about a little girl that sent Bibles to China. I thought if she could do that I could, too!*
> *But, I mostly did it for God. I collected $915.00, enough to buy 305 Bibles to send through ServLife.*
>
> *Sincerely,*
> *Jessica Carder, age 8*
> *Las Vegas, Nevada*

• **A Plane ride in India.** One summer while ministering in India, I was getting very low on cash after being in the country all summer. I had just one more week left and did not know how I was going to make it. I was very concerned and worried. I was traveling with a local pastor and we also needed to give some money to a pastor in Nepal who had just gotten out of prison so he could have some Bible training. I also needed funds for a bus ticket to Calcutta to fly back to America.

As we were on our plane ride, (we had bought the plane ticket two months before), the flight attendant announced they were going to do a drawing for 3,000 rupees (about $50). You're right! We won the drawing and had enough money to take care of the pastor we were about to see and get us on our way. The Bible says, "And my God will meet all your needs according to his glorious riches in Christ Jesus."[15]

• **A Fund Raiser in Nepal.** Our family is currently living in Nepal as I am writing this book (well, at least this chapter). A local Nepali church we attend is building a home for the elderly in Kathmandu, the capital. The land and building together are about $80,000. They encourage people to give for the project in the following way: if you have a motorcycle, give 5,000 rupees ($69); if you own a car, give 20,000 rupees ($273); and so forth. Because of this approach, the money has been raised! Just imagine what could be accomplished in American if we gave in a similar way: if you own your own home, give $1,000; if you have a second home, give $10,000; if you have a net worth of $1 million or more, give $50,000; etc. It's a simple idea, but it could put some spice in a fund raising project for local or global missions.

• **An extra BMW in Indiana.** I was meeting with a doctor for lunch in Indiana. He had come to realize God wanted him to sell his extra BMW and give the profit to our mission. As we talked about what it means to be a follower of Jesus, it became apparent that God was working in his heart about his material possessions. He was overwhelmed with the need for the continued growth and expansion of the Gospel in the world, especially in places where churches do not exist. It was clear he needed to sell this car. He informed me of this decision before I was able to share with him some financial needs of our ministry. Little did he know that I was about to ask him for a donation for our mission and that the amount I had in mind was exactly what he gained from the sale of his BMW. God does provide.

Questions for Personal Reflection or Small Group Study:

1. When have you experienced someone being generous in giving? How did that experience inspire you?

2. Share a time when you were moved to give your time or money to help someone in need. What is it that led you to act?

3. What did you grow up thinking about debt, and what is your view now on debt? Do you think it is okay for Christians to be in debt? Why or why not?

4. Try this exercise with your family, small group or Sunday school class. Give the money you collect to your church or a mission organization that is committed to making disciples of all nations and empowering the poor and oppressed:

- Give $5 if you have a roof over your head $_____
- Give $1 if your house is heated $_____
- Give $1 if you have air conditioning $_____
- Give $2 for every bed in your house $_____
- Give $5 for each indoor bathroom you have. $_____
- Give $1 for every phone in your house $_____
- Give $2 for every personal computer you own $_____
- Give $1 for every television in your house $_____
- Give $2 for each car you own $_____
- Give $0.01 for each item of clothing you own $_____
- Give $0.25 for each pair of shoes you own $_____
- Give $0.50 for every appliance you own $_____
- Give $0.01 for every dish in your kitchen $_____
- Give $0.50 for each meal you eat on an
  average day $_____
- Give $0.05 for every video tape you own $_____
- Give $0.10 for every CD or DVD you own $_____
- Give $0.50 for every year of school you have
  completed $_____
- Give $0.05 for every vitamin you take each day $_____
- Give $0.05 for each glass of water you drink
  per day $_____
- Give $0.50 for every shower you take per week $_____
- Give $0.25 for each hour you watch T.V. per day $_____
- Give $0.25 for each hour you spend online
  each day $_____
- Give $1 for each load of laundry you do
  each week. $_____
- Give $1 for every church activity you attend
  each month $_____

GRAND TOTAL $_____

Notes

1. see Matthew 16:24-25
2. James 2:5-6
3. Matthew 25
4. Ron Blue, "Generous Living: Finding Contentment through Giving," speech delivered at the annual Generous Giving Conference, Atlanta, Ga., January 14-15, 1999.
5. Matthew 28:19-20
6. Romans 15:24
7. Bill Bright, as quoted in *Generous Living: Finding Contentment through Giving* by Ron Blue with Jodie Berndt (Grand Rapids, Michigan: Zondervan Publishing House, 1997), 201
8. George Barna, Barna Research Archives: Money (Barna Research Group)
9. Missions Frontiers, July-August 2004
10. Acts 20:35
11. George Barna, *How to Increase Giving in Your Church: A Practical Guide to the Sensitive Task of Raising Money for Your Church or Ministry* (Ventura, California: Regal Books, 1997), 20
12. Hebrews 11:1
13. Hebrews 11:6
14. Philippians 4:11-13
15. Philippians 4:19

CHAPTER 5

Lessons on Prayer from a Nun

"If we never look at Him or think of what we owe Him and of the death which He suffered for our sakes, I do not see how we can get to know Him or do good works in His service. For what can be the value of faith without works, or works which are not united with the merit of our Lord Jesus Christ? And what but such thoughts can arouse us to love this Lord?"
—Teresa of Avila

"God did not make the first human because He needed company, but because He wanted someone to whom he could show His generosity and love. God did not tell us to follow Him because he needed our help, but because He knew that loving Him would make us whole."—Irenaeus

"Is prayer your steering wheel or your spare tire?"
—Corrie Ten Boom

While a student in college I helped organize a mission team to Calcutta, India. I had a burning desire to experience one of the poorest cities in the world. That might seem like a strange desire for a college student to have, but I believe God planted it my heart. There was a hunger in me to understand the Gospel in the context of a culture completely foreign to my own. I suspected that some of the ways I perceived and perhaps lived my Christian journey had been shaped more by my American culture than by Scripture. And I really wanted to be obedient to the words of Jesus to, "Go and make disciples of all nations."[1]

I had never been to India or organized a trip like this before, but I was thrilled at the opportunity! The city ranked with the lowest standard of urban living in the world was soon to be our destination. Our team, which started with more than 20 individuals, eventually dwindled down to just four. We were all young and inexperienced, yet ready to face harsh conditions and venture into a land completely alien to our understanding. Deep down, we all wanted to experience more of God than our narrow-minded suburban upbringing had shown us. We wanted to challenge the lies of the "American Dream"—the false beliefs that are perhaps not spoken overtly, but are certainly impressed upon many young people in American churches today. These beliefs include, "God wants you to be happy and safe," or "Being a Christian is just one aspect of your life—on the same level with your work life, your family life or your dating life."

These beliefs were taught and lived by many around me. However, there was a "disconnect" for me between these teachings and Jesus' call for us to take up our cross and follow Him to make disciples of all nations (see Matthew 16:24 and 18:19-20). I could not accept that God was solely concerned with my comfort and safety. There had to be more to the Christian journey than living the American Dream: go to college, get a job, live in the suburbs, raise a family, retire in a warm climate and die.

I was always intrigued with India. It's a place of contrasts: rich and poor; urban and rural; death and life; misery and joy. It's a land of religion, temples and a fervency of worship that truly humbled me when I saw it for the first time. People in India are not ashamed to express and devote themselves to idols and to rituals in their attempt to find identity, meaning and purpose for their lives. The land as a whole is difficult to get your hands around or to explain to anyone who hasn't been there. You have to experience it yourself—and even then, you will only scratch the surface of understanding.

Just taking those first few steps out of the airport challenged my western perceptions of life. For starters, there was a cow sitting next to my taxi in front of the airport—not a common encounter for most of us. Our driver kicked it several times to get it out of the way so we could leave.

The smells were odors I had never experienced. Most of them were far from pleasant or soothing. Garbage was piled up along the roadways in every direction. Most everyone used the street and parks as public toilets— definitely not a sight (or smell) often experienced in North America.

The day after we arrived, I decided to play a joke on my friends by telling them, "Hey, let's go visit a friend of mine in Calcutta." Actually, I was thinking of Mother Teresa (whom I had never met), but they had no idea who I was talking about. After getting strange and doubtful looks, we began walking. We trekked through the city for over 30 minutes until we came to the Mother House. There was a simple sign at the door that read, "Mother Teresa."

"Your friend is Mother Teresa?" my friends asked in amazement. The joke was over shortly, however, once a nun opened the door and we humbly requested to visit

Mother Teresa. We all were shocked when she said yes! I mean who would ever think this was possible? I thought only presidents, movie stars or wealthy people could have an audience with the most famous nun in the world.

When we entered the building, it was only about five minutes later when Mother Teresa came running out excited and energetic. She said, "Welcome to India! What brings you here?" And then she said, "Please have one of my business cards," handing us all one. It was amazing.

After visiting just a few minutes, one of the sisters came to us and said if we wanted a photo with her we should come back the next day. Of course we did go back. She greeted us with the same energy and enthusiasm; impressive for an old woman without shoes. Again she welcomed us to India, asking what we were doing there and handing out her business cards. It was like déjà vu. I wanted to say, "Mother, we were just here yesterday and told you who we are," but we gave her the benefit of the doubt. I later framed the business card she gave me, which she had signed with these words:

"The fruit of Silence is prayer
The fruit of prayer is faith
The fruit of Faith is Love
The fruit of Love is Service
The fruit of service is peace."
—Mother Teresa

A few days later, our team was on a train up to Darjelling, India to minister at a school. During the train ride I read the amazing story of Agnes Gonxha Bojaxhiu of Albania. Agnes was 16 when she left Albania to minister in India. Long before she won the Noble Prize for peace or before winning multiple honorary doctorate degrees from the most prestigious academic institutions in the world, this young woman followed God's call and left her home to share Christ's love in a far off land. When she first arrived, she took a position teaching English in a home for girls. Sometime later she was on a train ride, wrestling about what it was she thought God was really calling her to do, and she realized He was calling her to start her own ministry to the poorest of the poor in Calcutta.

When she went to her boss to ask if she could pursue this, he responded by saying, "What makes you think you can have your own ministry to the poor? You cannot even light the candles during mass. You are too young." Without letting this stop her, Agnes began ministering to the poor in Calcutta and the rest of her story is known by the world. Agnes later changed her name to Teresa, after Saint Teresa.

I met with Mother Teresa a few more times over the next four years, but the most significant and impacting conversation was during my fourth visit to her home.

It was only six months before her death—at the end of 1996. I had been in Cuba earlier that year and upon arrival in Havana, I saw two Sisters of Charity (Mother Teresa's order). They had the white saris with blue trimming and were easy to spot. I approached them and noticed they were from India, thus allowing me to practice my Hindi in Cuba. They both smiled and we spoke for several minutes.

"What are you doing in Cuba?" one lady asked. "We are here to share Christ's love with people!" I replied.

They both smiled again. I told them of my love for India and that I had visited India many times and had met "Mother," which is the way the sisters refer to her. One of the ladies looked at me intensely and said that if I went back to India I should tell Mother that their work in Cuba is going well and they send her their greetings. I thought very little of it at the time and did not believe this conversation would come up in the future, but it did. Later that year, I was in Calcutta and went to where Mother Teresa lived and worked. She was much different from the first time I met her. She was in a wheelchair and not the energetic person I had met several years before.

I remembered the encounter with the sisters in Cuba and leaned over and told her I had a message for her. I said I had been in Cuba a few months before and that her sisters told me to tell her their work was going well and they send their greetings and love. She seemed to really listen to me and cared what I had to say about these sisters in Cuba.

Then she looked up at me and asked, "Do you want to come with me to pray?" I said, "Of course!" She was pushed into a different room and I walked beside her. Not knowing what was going to happen next, she reached out her hands to me. I extended my hands and as she touched them she said, "This is how we teach all our sisters to pray..." She held my hands and touched each of my fingers in turn...

With your left hand:
1. I Can
2. I will
3. By God's grace
4. I will be
5. Holy

With your right hand:
1. You
2. Did
3. It
4. To
5. Me

These words are taken from Jesus in Matthew 25:40, "The King will reply, 'I tell you the truth, whatever you did for one of the least of these brothers of mine, you did for me."

She then said, "Put your hands together and pray." We then sat in a room and had prayer with the other sisters for about an hour. When we were done, she handed me the rosaries in her hands and told me to keep them. I thought, "Wow! She gave me her rosaries!" Then I thought she probably did not even own her own prayer beads and just wanted me to have some. Whatever the case was, I was happy to receive them.

Mother Teresa taught me something very beautiful that day about prayer, and I will never forget it. There is a mystery and a deep beauty to the role of prayer in the Christian life. Prayer embraces both a vertical and horizontal dimension to the Christian journey. The spiritual nurturing and growth of our lives as well as our ministry to the poor, lost and despised are woven together like two pieces of yarn. Discipleship and evangelism are married. Being and doing are somehow integrated in a holistic manner. Like breathing is to the human body, prayer is essential to us as followers of Jesus to both our spiritual growth and our service to others.

That day with Mother Teresa was a day that is marked in my "spiritual memories" Hall of Fame. C.S. Lewis said, "Truth is not created, it is discovered." And that day, the discovery was profound. I had discovered something beautiful in the realization that my spiritual growth is always connected to my service and love for other people. My service to others is not essential for knowing God, but my service to others is keenly linked to my growing in God.

After reflecting on a few familiar Scriptures, I realized how key the vertical and horizontal dimensions of our Christian journeys really are. James says that faith without works is dead (James 2:17). In Ephesians 2:8, the Apostle Paul explains that salvation is a gift from God, but just a few verses later he adds that we are God's workmanship, created in Christ Jesus to do good works. Jesus says the greatest commandment is to love God with all your heart, soul and mind *and* to love your neighbor as yourself (Matthew 22:37-39).

We will not grow and mature in our spiritual journey until we connect the vertical and horizontal together. The Christian life is about how we learn to love God *and* love people. What we do in prayer, in service to others and in our commitment to community impacts our ability to grow and be transformed into the image of Jesus Christ—which is the goal of discipleship. Some people may want to come to Christ and receive the free gift of salvation and not be concerned with giving their time, money or energy to love those around them or across the globe. But choosing such an approach can never lead to genuine transformation because it's only half of the equation. Jesus has called us to believe in Him *and* to do good works.

The Role of Prayer in Transformation

Engaging in prayer that connects both the vertical and horizontal dimensions of the Christian life is crucial to growing and being formed into Christ's image. This sort of prayer focuses our attention on the world around us, yet keeps our dependency upon God and not on our own human ability. For if we rely on our human ability or intellect, then we are not truly relying on God to do in us and through us what He alone can do. There are two passages of Scripture that offer insight.

We proclaim him, admonishing and teaching everyone with all wisdom, so that we may present everyone perfect in Christ.

To this end I labor, struggling with all his energy, which so powerfully works in me.[2]

and

Now to him who is able to do immeasurably more than all we ask or imagine, according to his power that is at work within us, to him be glory in the church and in Christ Jesus throughout all generations, for ever and ever! Amen.[3]

When I asked Mother Teresa more about prayer, she told me, "Prayer enlarges the heart, until it is capable of containing the gift of God Himself." God wants us to know Him and to desire Him.

A.W. Tozer said, "God wants to be wanted." All of us want to be wanted, loved and known by someone. It is the deepest cry of the human experience. So does God. God wants people to hunger for him as they hunger for their favorite meal after a day without eating at all. The unfortunate truth is, many times we don't want God. Or else we don't want the things God wants, such as hatred of sin (Psalms 45:7; 97:10; 101:3 and Proverbs 8:13); justice for the poor (Psalms 140:12; 102:17); and all people and nations knowing and worshiping Him (2 Peter 3:9 and 1 Timothy 2:4).

A change needs to happen in our hearts, and that change begins with prayer and in realizing that authentic communion with God will result in the horizontal expression of humble service to others. It has always fascinated me that the one request the disciples made of Jesus was, "Lord, teach us to pray."[4] It was not, "Teach us how to do miracles like you do," or "Teach us how to craft a clever sermon," or "Teach us how to understand culture." They saw through Jesus' example that prayer was at the center of it all... "But Jesus often withdrew to lonely places and prayed."[5]

Many people I talk to, even church leaders, do not understand prayer. I was once at a church pastors' conference in America listening to a leader confess he did not know how to teach on prayer. I confess that I, too, have much to learn about prayer and want to learn from the people of God who have walked before me—many of whom seem to have amazing intimacy with God through their prayer lives.

The lives and writings of Brother Lawrence, A.W. Tozer, Teresa of Avila, C.S. Lewis, John Wesley, Richard Foster and Dallas Willard have all been invaluable to me. Through their examples, as well as my own experience, I have learned many things about prayer. But one of the most important is this—that abundant living and fruitful ministry, no matter what kind of ministry, must be fueled and sustained through a life of prayer.

Here are some practical suggestions on ways you can nurture a sense of communion with God through prayer:

• **Nature**—As you walk, bike or drive in your car allow the beauty of God's creation to awaken your communion with Him. Thank Him for the beauty He created and ask Him to awaken the creative within you as you long to experience Him.

• **Personal Suffering**—C.S. Lewis wrote, "God whispers in our joys, speaks to us in our conscience, but shouts to us in our pain." As you experience pain in your life through the death of someone you love, a loss of a relationship, or some other circumstance, ask God to allow you to embrace the pain and use it to understand how God hurts for the lost and broken. How you approach and work through the pain in your life, it will shape how you help others heal from their pain.

• **Solitude**—Quietness is the basic premise of solitude and should be viewed as a doorway into communion with God. Times of solitude can be intentional and also welcomed when brought about by circumstance, such as when you are driving in the car or working on a project alone.

• **Silence**—Soren Kierkegaard wrote, "A man prayed, and at first he thought that prayer was talking. But he became more and more quiet until in the end he realized that prayer is listening." *Prayer is communication.* To have effective communication between two people, one speaks and one listens. When we learn to listen to the voice of Jesus in our prayer life through observing intentional silence, our prayer life will take on deeper meaning and growth. Jesus said, "My sheep will know my voice."[6]

• **Art**—While in Amsterdam on a layover, I visited the Rikes Museum. There I observed a painting from the Renaissance Period on the Nativity and the birth of Jesus. In the painting, all three wise men came from different nations and ethnic groups. One carried incense coming from Asia. Another came from Africa possessing gold, and a third, an Arab, carried myrrh. I was moved by the artist's message—that from the very beginning of Jesus' life, all nations and tribes were created to worship Him and know Him (Revelation 7:9). Through viewing a work of art, watching a film or observing a play, you can discover a deeper truth for your Christian journey or led to acknowledge how great God is and worship Him.

• **Relationships**—Whether dating or marriage, relationships are difficult and provide ample opportunity to move toward God in prayer.

- **Community**—By having community and deepening friendships with other Christians, you can learn to pray together for each others' needs.
- **Work**—The workplace is a mission field. Through your job you can pray for increased wisdom on how to love people the way Christ would love them and how to be a light in a dark place.
- **Travel**—By traveling to other countries and experiencing diverse cultures, your heart will be moved to deeper levels of intercession for the people and circumstances you encounter. As you walk through the streets of cities and towns, you can pray for the Gospel to advance.
- **Suffering of Others**—As you engage with people who are suffering, your compassion is awakened and your prayer life deepened.
- **Evil**—As you expand your awareness to see the evil in your own society and in other societies, you will be compelled to pray and to seek God for ways to intervene and to be a voice for justice and truth. Evils such as child labor, drug trafficking, genocide and corporate greed and corruption are a few examples.

Different Ways to Engage in Prayer

Author Meister Eckhart offers wise advice when he says that styles do not bring change, rather, God does.[7] There is no magic formula to how we should pray, and we should not fall in the trap of believing that a particular method of prayer is the "right" or "best" way to bend God's ear. There are many ways to pray, and most all of them have something of value to offer us in our spiritual journey. Here are some of the different approaches to prayer that have been meaningful in my own journey:

- **Meditation**—Simply meditating on a verse of Scripture or a word (such as "love" or "forgiveness") has often led me into the presence of God. If I am meditating on the word love, for example, I begin to pray and ask God to show me more of His love for me and to thank Him for the times He has shown me His love in the past. Then I begin to meditate on how I can better love others.

• *Lectio Divina*—This Latin phrase means "into the presence of God through the text." As you read and study texts of Scripture, pray to enter and experience the presence of God.

• **Prayer Walking**—Prayer walking simply means to pray while walking. You can do it alone or with a partner. Perhaps you can pray Scripture together or pray for the neighborhoods and people you pass as you go by. Prayer walking can also be an effective form of spiritual warfare in cities or countries where people do not know God.

• **Repetitive Phrases**—Often a repetitive phrase can help lead you into God's presence in prayer—such as "God is my refuge" or "His mercy endures forever." As you repeat these biblical truths over and over, you allow the Holy Spirit to speak to you and to fill you with understanding.

• **The Psalms**—Read, pray and sing the psalms. Whenever I am in another country or church service in another language, I always sing along with the church, replacing the words I don't understand with words from a psalm.

• **Warfare**—The metaphor of war is a powerful one to think through when you are faced with impossible odds or circumstances. More about this in Chapter 9.

• **A.C.T.S.**—This acronym could perhaps guide you in prayer:

Adoration—Give praise to God for who He is, what He has done, and what He is going to do.

121

Confession—Confess your sins and mistakes and God who is faithful will hear your prayer and forgive you (1 John 1:9).

Thanksgiving—Thank God for what He has done in your life, for your family and for the blessings He has given you.

Supplication—Pray for other people you love and know. Pray for missionaries, pray for your church, your pastor and the work of the church around the world.

• **The Lord's Prayer**—Memorize, speak and study the prayer Jesus used to teach His disciples how to pray. I often pray this prayer to lead me into the presence of God.

> *This, then, is how you should pray:*
> *"Our Father in heaven,*
> *hallowed be your name,*
> *your kingdom come,*
> *your will be done*
> *on earth as it is in heaven.*
> *Give us today our daily bread.*
> *Forgive us our debts,*
> *as we also have forgiven our debtors.*
> *And lead us not into temptation,*
> *but deliver us from the evil one."*[8]

The Results of Prayer

Prayer is not just for our own blessing, but for the transformation of other people and nations. God hears the prayers of His people and responds accordingly. Prayer has impact! When we pray:

• **God is honored.** The goal of our prayers should be that God will be exalted in every circumstance, decision or trial so all nations and peoples on earth will come to know him. "'My name will be great among the nations, from the rising to the setting of the sun. In every place incense and pure offerings will be brought to my name because my name will be great among the nations," says the Lord Almighty."[9] We often are rushed to prayer in hard times and stressful circumstances. However, prayer is not merely about our needs or wants, but about God receiving glory throughout all the earth.

• **I am changed.** As we see the fruit of prayer in our lives, God will change us and reveal to us Himself. "And we, who with unveiled faces all reflect the Lord's glory, are being transformed into His likeness with ever-increasing glory, which comes from the Lord, who is the Spirit."[10]

• **Families and relationships are changed.** As we live a life of prayer, forgiveness happens, hurts are forgotten and relationships are healed and transformed into healthy, vibrant and dynamic expressions of faith. As the old saying goes, "Families that pray together, stay together!"

• **Churches are changed.** The body of Christ is made of broken people who desire to be healed and transformed. The instrument of that healing and transformation is prayer. As Jesus said, "My house shall be called a house of prayer for all the nations."[11] As we commit to prayer as individuals and families, this commitment will flow into our local churches. Churches will be filled with people who are filled with the Holy Spirit and who love, serve and give of themselves.

• **Cities are changed.** As individuals, families and churches are transformed and live for God's glory, then their cities will change. Crime will decrease, the poor will be helped to stand on their own, neglected children will be cared for and encouraged to stay in school, widows will be served, and broken people will be loved and healed.

• **Nations are changed.** As change happens in individuals, families, churches and communities, whole nations will bring glory to God through administering justice and caring for the orphan and the widow and the poor.

I want to close this chapter with a real life example of the powerful impact a single person's prayer life can have on a nation. The famous missionary, William Carey, left England in the 19th Century for India. His life of prayer and dedication to God served as a catalyst for major changes in Indian society. However, it did not come easy. Carey did not go to school beyond age 12 when he became a cobbler's apprentice. Most would say he was educationally unqualified to be a missionary.

By 24, Carey was preparing for his ordination and was rejected when he gave his first sermon as a candidate. It took two more years for him to be ordained to the ministry. He did not give up and kept praying that God would allow him to be a missionary. Carey's missionary concern was ignored until 1792 when he produced one of the most important books in all of church history: *An Enquiry into the Obligations of Christians.* He was 31 years old.

In it he argued that The Great Commission in Matthew 28:19-20 was not just solely to the apostles in the Bible, but to Christians of all periods. It proved to be a kind of charter for the modern Protestant missionary movement. His colleagues formed a missionary society and sent Carey as their first missionary to India. Carey and his wife, Dorothy, lost three small children to disease in India. Dorothy progressively lost her sanity there and could not cope with the strain of living at a subsistence level. It was prayer that kept Carey going.

Carey spent seven years in India before seeing anyone come to Christ, but he never stopped praying. One of the obstacles to conversion in India was the persecution of anyone who became a Christian as it meant breaking caste. Other practices Carey had to oppose as a Christian and which slowed down the progress of Christian conversion were sacrificing children to the gods and burning widows alive on their husband's funeral pyres.

Inspired through prayer, William Carey became a leading voice against the unjust Hindu practice of *Sati*, cremating a woman beside the body of her dead husband. As a result of his influence, the Indian government eventually made Sati illegal in 1829.

Official opposition from the British East India Company which did not want missionaries in India didn't help either. Then there was a disastrous fire at the mission printing plant in 1812 that destroyed years of Carey's translation work. There were repeated attacks of malaria and cholera, impoverished living conditions and insufficient funds to survive. Carey had to take up other employment just to survive.

How did he make it? I would say it was through a life of prayer. He translated the Bible into 34 languages and encyclopedias into local languages; helped import the printing press; compiled dictionaries of Sanskrit, Marathi, Punjabi and Telegu—respected today as authoritative; started the still influential Serampore College; began churches and established 19 mission stations; formed 100 rural schools, encouraging the education of girls; started the Horticultural Society of India; served as professor at Fort William College, Calcutta; began the weekly publication, *"The Friend of India"* (continued today as *"The Statesman"*); printed the first Indian newspaper; and introduced the concept of the savings bank to assist poor farmers.[12]

His life of prayer and perseverance has inspired tens of thousands to give themselves for the spread of the

Gospel. Carey's story is impressive, but it need not be unique. Miraculous things will happen through us, too, if we simply commit ourselves to prayer.

Questions for Personal Reflection or Small Group Study:

1. What circumstance have you faced that have resulted in a growth in your prayer life?

2. How might your understanding of the Gospel of Jesus Christ be wrongfully influenced by American culture?

3. Based on the list used by the author, what are two ways you can enhance your prayer life this month?

4. How are the "vertical" and "horizontal" dimensions of prayer life being expressed through your life?

5. Perhaps write down or share with someone 3 people you can pray for on a daily basis. Also, list 2 countries of the world you can begin praying for daily.

Notes

1. Matthew 28:19
2. Colossians 1:28-29
3. Ephesians 3:20-21
4. Luke 11:1
5. Luke 5:16
6. John 10:27
7. Eckhart, as quoted by J. Heinrich Arnold in *Discipleship: Living for Christ in the Daily Grind* (Plough Publishing House, Farmington, PA, 1991), 24
8. Matthew 6:9-13
9. Malachi 1:11
10. 2 Corinthians 3:18
11. Mark 11:17
12. www.gospelcom.net

CHAPTER
6

It Starts with Compassion

"The 'least of my brethren' are the hungry and the lonely, not only for food, but for the Word of God; the thirsty and the ignorant not only for water, but also for knowledge, peace, truth, justice and love; the naked and the unloved, not only for clothes but also for human dignity; the unwanted; the unborn child; the racially discriminated against; the homeless and abandoned, not only for a shelter made of bricks, but for a heart that understands, that covers, that loves; the sick, the dying destitute, and the captives, not only in body, but also in mind and spirit; all those who have lost all hope and faith in life; the alcoholics and dying addicts and all those who have lost God (for them God was but God is) and who have lost all hope in the power of the Spirit."—Mother Teresa

"May I become at all times, both now and forever
A protector for those without protection
A guide for those who have lost their way
A ship for those with oceans to cross
A bridge for those with rivers to cross
A sanctuary for those in danger
A lamp for those without light
A place of refuge for those who lack shelter
And a servant to all in need."—Unknown

He was 21 years old when he went to China with an upstart missionary agency. "What can I do?" he asked himself. "I am so young. Everyone says I am too young to venture out to a far off land where I've never been." He was not detoured by the criticism of those around him, however. He would not let his age stop him from following God's call and his deep compassion for the lost in the world. He was eager to share Christ with the people of China. His compassion did not stop at merely feeling empathy for the people of China, but would eventually lead him to give his life for them.

At the time he went to China, it was illegal for foreigners to enter the interior of the country. He could only travel to the port cities. But his heart was filled with so much compassion for the people of China that he ignored this law and made his way into the heart of the nation. He later wrote back home these words, "At home, you can never know what it is to be absolutely alone, amidst thousands, everyone looking on you with curiosity, with contempt, with suspicion, or with dislike. Thus to learn what it is to be despised and rejected of men... and then to have the love of Jesus applied to your heart by the Holy Spirit... this is precious, this is worth coming for."

The year was 1857, and the man was J. Hudson Taylor. We know him today, but very few people knew him at that early age. He was a pioneer—a young man who had a vision inspired by the Holy Spirit. Funds from home rarely arrived, but Taylor was determined to rely upon God for his every need, and he never appealed for money to his friends in England. Repeatedly he later told others, "Depend upon it. God's work, done in God's way, will never lack for supplies."

One day a man asked Taylor to explain why he had buttons on the back of his coat. Taylor then realized his western style of dress was distracting his listeners from his message, so he decided to dress like a Mandarin, a Chinese teacher. He was amazed at how dressing Chinese allowed him to travel more freely and be accepted more readily by the people. Taylor's goal was not to have the Chinese become like English Christians, but to have them become Chinese Christians.

The sufferings and hardships multiplied: Taylor's daughter died from water on the brain; the family was almost killed in the Yang Chow Riot of 1868; Maria, Taylor's first wife, died while giving birth; his second wife died of cancer; sickness and ill health were frequent. Yet, the China Inland Mission continued its work of reaching China's millions for Christ. By 1895 the Mission had 641 missionaries plus 462 Chinese helpers at 260 stations. Under Hudson Taylor's leadership, China Inland Mission had supplied over half of the Protestant missionary force in China. During the Boxer Rebellion of 1900, 56 of these missionaries were martyred, and hundreds of Chinese Christians were killed. The missionary work did not slack, however, and the number of missionaries quadrupled in the coming decades.[1]

Compassion is absolutely essential for anyone who wants to make an impact on other people—no matter if those people are in our own communities or on the other side of the globe. For some of us compassion comes easy. We see someone in physical pain or emotionally hurting and we feel compassion for them. For others, however, compassion does not come easily. I am sure we all know people who respond to human suffering with apathy and anger and give little care for the poor, oppressed and marginalized. When they see a starving child on television, perhaps they get angry and think, "This group puts these images on television just to make me feel bad. I have enough troubles of my own as it is. I can't be expected to solve the world's problems too, can I?"

In the back of our minds, we all know that suffering is real in the world, but sometimes it's hard not to respond with frustration when the images of suffering come spilling into our living rooms week after week. What good does it really do for these groups to shove these images in our faces? What can we really do to make a dent in the suffering that seems so pervasive across the world?

For many of us who are followers of Jesus Christ, we have missed the biblical understanding of compassion. I often meet Buddhists, Hindus, Muslims or Jews who demonstrate more biblical compassion for the oppressed than some Christians I meet.

Surely, if the risen Christ lives in us, we should follow the model of Jesus and have compassion that is always connected to action. Biblical compassion is not merely feeling pity for someone. Surely, anyone can do this. But as God works in us we desire to step out and touch people with our words and actions to demonstrate the love of Jesus Christ to an individual, a community or a nation.

How do we get that kind of compassion for the lost, the suffering and the oppressed? How can we grow in the kind of compassion that will move the heart of God?

Jesus gives us the answer. Ministry is basically responding to compassion as Jesus modeled throughout the Scriptures. Consider this story from His life, which is recorded in the Gospels of Matthew, Mark and Luke:

> *A man with leprosy came to him and begged him on his knees, "If you are willing, you can make me clean."*
> *Filled with compassion, Jesus reached out his hand and touched the man. "I am*

*willing," he said. "Be clean" Immediately
the leprosy left him and he was cured.*

*Jesus sent him away at once with a
strong warning: "See that you don't tell
this to anyone. But go, show yourself to
the priest and offer the sacrifices that
Moses commanded for your cleansing, as
a testimony to them." Instead he went out
and began to talk freely, spreading the
news. As a result, Jesus could no longer
enter a town openly but stayed outside in
lonely places. Yet the people still came to
him from everywhere.*[2]

Compassion Starts with Looking and Listening

In this familiar story of Jesus we see a beautiful
model for how compassion for others should lead us. The
man with leprosy came to Jesus and spoke to Him—and,
at first, Jesus simply listened. He was aware of this man's
suffering and humility, and though He may have been
preoccupied with His own agenda for the day, He was
willing to stop and make Himself aware of the suffering
before Him. What does it mean for us to listen in this
way? What does it mean to really see what is going on?

On one level, this "listening compassion" starts
wherever we live and with whomever we come across.
Whether in our home, in the classroom, or at work, we
can listen to those around us who express their pain or
perhaps hide their pain behind their busyness or a smile.
Only through listening in this way can our compassion
be awakened. If we do not have a heart for the lost and
the poor, it means we are not looking and listening. In
many ways, this book is about how God has taught me to
listen and look at people throughout the world who do

not know God and how out of that, compassion has emerged.

This "listening compassion" can also extend to the world at large. September 11, 2001 was a clear indication for all Americans on this issue. It was interesting to see a pattern develop among different parts of the country and different generations towards this horrible event. Some became more patriotic and wanted to buy more American flags to hang on their front porches or on the radio antennas on their cars. Others became more curious and wanted to understand why so much hatred towards America exists. Some just asked, "Who did this?" while others asked, "Why did this happen?"

I think younger generations tended to ask the why question and became more globally aware, while the older generations became more patriotic. Still others responded with greater apathy and passivity toward the world and still did not understand their role in the global community.

How can we as the church come to a posture of listening and really hear what is going on in the world? It all begins by following the model of Jesus to see and to listen to those in need around us, and then extend that compassion to those who live far away.

The world today is filled with suffering. The distance between the "haves" and the "have nots" is growing. Poverty, disease, war and injustice leave millions of people without access to food, water, basic health care, education and access to hearing the Gospel. Today, there are more than 30 wars going on across the globe and millions of people who live with very little possibility of even meeting a Christian because there are not many around. Here are a few brief statistics to put things in perspective:

- Forty-two million people are now living with HIV/AIDS. In Botswana alone, an appalling 35 percent of the adult population is living with HIV/ AIDS.[3]

• More than 1 billion live in absolute poverty. This includes 700 million people living in slums, 500 people on the verge of starvation, 93 million beggars, and 200 million children exploited for labor.[4]

• A majority of people alive today do not know the Savior. This includes 1.19 billion Muslims, 811 million Hindus, 360 million Buddhists, 228 million ethno-religionists, 23 million Sikhs, 14 million Jews, 768 million agnostics, and 150 million atheists.[5]

Compassion Involves Feeling

Filled with compassion, Jesus reached out his hand and touched the man. "I am willing," he said. "Be clean!" Immediately the leprosy left him and he was cured.[6]

I have stood in refugee camps in Africa, garbage cities in Cairo and among the untouchables in India, and I have been filled with this pain that resides in me. It does not come often. But when it does, God is speaking and present.

The Greek word for compassion is *splagchnizomai* (splangkh-nid'-zom-ahee), which means "to have the bowels yearn, i.e. (figuratively) feel sympathy, to pity."[7] For Jesus, compassion meant there was a physical reaction in His stomach. We should pray that God fills us with a compassion that allows us to be physically affected.

I remember the first time I experienced compassion on this level. I was walking down the streets in Calcutta, India. The city that's ranked with the lowest standard of urban living in the world is filled with millions of people who live on the streets. On one occasion, I walked across the street because I was unable to continue walking where I was due to the dozens of bodies lying on the road. They were lying in human excrement. Some looked as if they were close to death, and most were naked and malnourished. The smell and the image haunts me to this day. The reaction in me was too much to process, and I began to weep as I had to walk around this group of people to get where I was going. I then saw I was across the street from one of Mother Teresa's homes for the dying. These villagers had been brought to Calcutta, some on their own and some brought by family to Mother Teresa's home to die in dignity.

God created emotion for a reason. Yet I see two mistakes in how we often process our emotions. First, for many of us, we do not integrate our emotion with our faith, for whatever reason. We might have heard, "Choosing Jesus should not be an emotional decision." We then try to separate emotion from our faith and practice our faith only in a cognitive, pragmatic and rational way. We are fine and affirmed in exercising our emotion in other areas of our lives: getting angry at our golf game, crying at a movie, or laughing at a sitcom, but when it comes to using our emotion in a way that moves us into commitment or action in our faith, we are often hesitant.

Another mistake we make is in the opposite extreme. We place too much emphasis on our emotions and refuse to take action unless we "feel like it." I have heard many times, "I don't read my Bible because I don't feel like it." Or "I did not share my faith with my friend because it did not feel right." We know clearly through Scripture that God wants us to study His Word and be active in sharing our faith whether we feel like it or not (Philemon 1:6). God created all of us as emotional beings and He wants to use our emotion to lead us to actions that might seem foolish to the world but will bring honor to Him.

Compassion Always Leads to Action

I overheard a conversation one time in which a man was talking about his friend's compassionate spirit. "Susan really has a lot of compassion for her friend," he said, "because she really is sad for her all the time."

Biblical compassion, however, is more than just a feeling. It provokes us to action. As Jesus demonstrates in the story of healing the leper, true compassion leads us to do something to alleviate the suffering we see. What action we take depends on our gifting, and will be different for all of us. For some reading this, it will mean leaving the mundane and unfulfilling job you have and move to another culture to give the love of Jesus Christ to a people who have seldom even met a follower of Jesus Christ.

For some it will mean selling your extra home or other luxuries to free up money to give to the cause of Christ. Still others will become intercessors and commit to pray for the advancement of the Gospel and the Church throughout the world.

I recently came across a ministry in Kathmandu, Nepal that filled me with hope and inspiration. An Indian man had gathered the disabled of Nepal together. There are about 35 who live in his "Prayer Tower," as they call it. Nepal provides no kind of government help to the handicapped, so most of the handicapped are outcasts of society, and the majority Hindu population views them as "cursed" by the gods. They believe they did a bad deed in their former life.

These disabled men and women have come to this ministry center solely to pray. Twenty-four hours a day, seven days a week, they take two-hour shifts and continually lift up prayers to God. The people I talked to there said to me, "My life is filled with purpose now. My compassion for my country is being put into action because now I can do something about it." No one is incapable of acting out of compassion.

Compassion is Concerned with Making People Productive Members of Society

Jesus sent him away at once with a strong warning: "See that you don't tell this to anyone. But go, show yourself to the priest and offer the sacrifices that Moses commanded for your cleansing, as a testimony to them" Instead he went out and began to talk freely, spreading the news. As a result, Jesus could no longer enter a town openly but stayed outside in lonely places. Yet the people still came to him from everywhere. [8]

Biblical compassion does not merely offer help to someone once and then not continue to be concerned about what happens to them after that. Jesus was not only concerned with healing the man's disease, He was concerned with his life as a whole. I believe we can learn two lessons from Jesus when it comes to using our compassion in a productive way.

• **Spiritual Restoration.** Most importantly, we should be concerned that people are spiritually restored to God through Christ. Second Peter 3:9 says, "The Lord is not slow in keeping his promise, as some understand slowness. He is patient with you, not wanting anyone to perish, but everyone to come to repentance." We must realize that God wants everyone in your school, your office, your family and the world to know Jesus Christ as Lord and Savior. This is the greatest gift we as followers of Christ have to offer. When our compassion leads us to action for others we should always keep this in mind and be concerned about others' salvation. We cannot act with compassion without remembering Paul's words, "...be prepared to give an answer to everyone who asks you to give the reason for the hope that you have. But do this with gentleness and respect."[9]

- **Societal Restoration.** There are societal implications when it comes to living out the Gospel. When our compassion leads us to help orphans in the world, it is not enough to simply share the message of Christ with them verbally and do nothing else. Compassion compels us to also see that they have opportunities to be loved, fed, clothed and educated. In the same way, when our compassion leads us to love victims of HIV/AIDS, we are compelled to create ways for victims to be cared for so they can become productive members of their communities. Of course, exactly what it looks like to help someone become a productive member of society will change depending on the person and the circumstance. There is no "one answer" for everyone. We must follow the leading of the Holy Spirit and seek the counsel from others. Imagine the different implications of bringing restoration to diverse groups such as convicts, orphans, drug addicts, prostitutes, college graduates, children or an unreached nomadic people group with no nation-state of their own.

I love what James writes: "What good is it, my brothers, if a man claims to have faith but has no deeds? Can such faith save him? Suppose a brother or sister is without clothes and daily food. If one of you says to him,

'Go, I wish you well; keep warm and well fed,' but does nothing about his physical needs, what good is it? In the same way, faith by itself, if it is not accompanied by action, is dead. But someone will say, 'You have faith; I have deeds.' Show me your faith without deeds, and I will show you my faith by what I do. You believe that there is one God. Good! Even the demons believe that—and shudder."[10]

What James means is that we must be holistic in our compassion. We should not simply preach the Gospel without loving people in practical ways, and at the same time we do not just love people without preaching the Gospel. I believe God is raising up a new generation of Christ followers who want to *demonstrate* and *proclaim* the Gospel to the world. For this new generation, there is no difference between embodying the Gospel in one's lifestyle and speaking the message of hope to those around the world who do not know God. As Jesus said, "I must preach the good news of the Kingdom of God to the other towns also, because that is why I was sent."[11]

"Some wish to live within the sound of Church or Chapel bells; I want to run a Rescue Shop within a yard of hell." The man who said this was 24 when his compassion for the poor and lost made him leave for China to join Hudson Taylor. His name was C.T. Studd, and the year was 1885. Like Taylor, Studd did not let his age stop him from serving Jesus and giving his whole life in service to God. His compassion did more than cause him to feel sorry for the people around the world; it provoked him to action.

Others told him he was too young to go to China. "What do you have to offer? You are just a young man," many said. But he knew God was calling him and that he must obey. Little did he know at the time that he would eventually become a rich man—in more ways than one.

Some time later, Studd's father died and left him a large inheritance. He chose to give away his inheritance to George Mueller in England, who was running orphanages and other ministries. Concerning that choice, he later wrote, "If Jesus Christ be God and died for me, then no sacrifice can be too great for me to make for Him."

Eventually, Studd traveled from China to minister in India and Sudan, which was the largest unreached area of the world at that time. Many accused him of being too zealous for God and his sharing the Gospel around the world. To that, he replied, "How could I spend the best years of my life in living for the honors of this world, when thousands of souls are perishing every day?"[12]

Questions for Personal Reflection or Small Group Study:

1. Does compassion come easily for you? Why or why not?

2. What is the most profound or memorable moment when you experienced compassion for a person or group of people? Describe it.

3. How might you create opportunities for others to grow in biblical compassion?

4. How can you grow in gaining more compassion in your Christian journey?

5. What are some other moments in the life of Jesus where He exercised compassion?

6. Where else in the Bible can you find powerful examples of compassion in action?

Notes
1. Ken Curtis PH.D., Beth Jacobson, Diana Severance Ph.D., Ann T. Snyder and Dan Graves, *GLIMPSES (Christian History Institute,* Worcester, PA, 1991)
2. Mark 1:40-45
3. The Wall Street Journal Europe, March 14, 2003
4. David B. Barrett and Todd M. Johnson, *World Christian Trends AD 30-AD 2000: Interpreting the Annual Christian Megacensus* (William Carey Library, Pasadena, CA, 2001), 34
5. David B. Barrett and Todd M. Johnson, *World Christian Trends AD 30-AD 2000: Interpreting the Annual Christian Megacensus,* 551
6. Mark 1:41-42
7. *Biblesoft's New Exhaustive Strong's Numbers and Concordance with Expanded Greek-Hebrew Dictionary.* (Biblesoft and International Bible Translators, Inc., 1994)
8. Mark 1:43-45
9. 1 Peter 3:15
10. James 2:14-19
11. Luke 4:43
12. Ken Curtis, Ph.D., and Diana Severance, Ph.D., *GLIMPSES (Christian History Institute, Worcester, PA, 1991)*

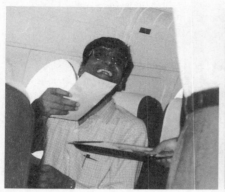

God providing in an amazing way:
pages 104-105

Nuraj and Ramesh at ServLife Children's
Home in India: page 169

After our rafting adventure: pages 23-24

Gune: Page 176

Zayd enjoying a woman's conference sponsored by ServLife 2003

Christian women praying in Nepal

Oxen being donated to local pastors from Sudan as a means to support their ministries and families

Merina lives at the ServLife children's home in Kathmandu, Nepal

Sadus are considered to be Hindu holy men

Boys at ServLife's Orphanage in Raxaul, India 2004

The first year of ServLife's orphananage 1997

ServLife India's director, Albert Das, prays for Hindu women who seeks healing: 1/2004

ServLife missionary reading the Bible: 4/2004

Elise and Zayd in Kathmandu, Nepal 12/2004

Saharawi refugees in Algeria: Page 190

Deepak in Raxaul, India

The day a man asked me to pray for his leg: Page 218

Our family driving
through India 2004

First training conference
for ServLife pastors

Working with indigenous churches in southern Thailand: 1/2005

Delivering Aid and sharing the gospel to Tsunami victims in southern Thailand: 1/2005

Children enjoying themselves in Bihar, India

Preaching at a church in southern California meeting on the beach/ I often define our ministry like this, "God takes us to the developing world to comfort the afflicted and then back to America to afflict the comforted."

Ashish praying at ServLife India's daily devotional time

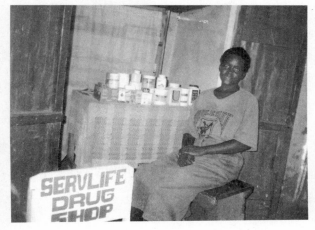

Empowering widows from Sudan through creating small businesses

Worship time at a ServLife Africa
Leadership Conference 2003

A man in Nepal

Children's Choir at Orphanage in India

Sudan choir sings
in refugee camps

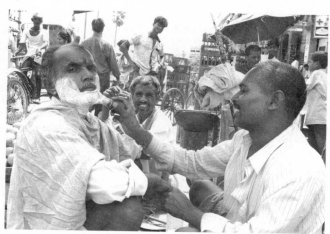

A man enjoys a
shave in Bihar,
India

A father and son
moment 10/2004

Zayd enjoying his friends at the orphanage in India 12/2004

A Dalit girl in India: page 192

Children at ServLife's Orphanage in India

CHAPTER 7

The Way Up is Down

"The great paradox which Scripture reveals to us is that real and total freedom can only be found through downward mobility... The divine way is indeed the downward way."
—Henri Nouwen

"No one can get up to that far crest unless he first goes down to the valley below. For our way leads downward...Christ showed this himself."
—St. Augustine of North Africa, the 4ᵗʰ-Century Bishop of Hippo

I've led a pretty unorthodox life since I got out of college. The phrase "shallow tent pegs" best described my life as a single man and continues to describe it today as a family man. In 2004 alone, my wife, son and I have lived in four cities in three different nations. So you can imagine as a single man, up to age 29, I was highly mobile and constantly traveled in order to do ministry around the world.

As you might expect, meeting my wife, our dating experience and our engagement were all pretty unorthodox as well. Elise and I met in Orlando at a conference where we had both been asked to speak. Although we did not start to date until a few months later, I immediately recognized that she had a heart for Jesus and the world unlike anyone I had ever met. I was content being single, and most of my family and close friends thought I would stay that way for the rest of my life. At the very least, because of my lifestyle, I knew God would have to work in miraculous ways to bring me a soul mate for life.

Our dating and engagement all happened long distance. I moved to Colorado just three days before we were married. It is not the sort of courtship process I would recommend to anyone else, but it is how it happened for us.

At one point during our engagement I went to visit Elise in Colorado and she began to complain about extreme pain in her side. As the pain increased, I decided to take her to the emergency room, fearing it was her appendix. Upon examination, the doctors found an eight-centimeter cyst on her ovaries. After more tests, her doctor told her the news no patient wants to hear, "You will need to go to the cancer center because there is a chance that the cyst is malignant." We made visits to the Denver cancer center, anticipating surgery to remove the cyst. This painful and stressful time came to a climax one evening when she looked up and asked, "If I do have cancer and they say I only have one year to live, do you want to still get married?"

I could not believe the question or the circumstance we were facing. It was the kind of situation you read about in books; it seemed unreal. I looked at Elise and said, "I love you and want to marry you even if we get to spend just one year together."

Thankfully, the cyst was successfully removed and there was no cancer. However, during the surgery the doctor punctured her bladder and, as a result, she had to be fitted with a catheter to drain off her fluids while the bladder healed. That was just two weeks before our wedding.

For those who don't know what this device is, it is usually what old people have to wear: a small bag, to hold your urine. We did not know whether it was going to be removed before our wedding day. It was a very stressful time. There was so much unknown, and we were both fearful about what might happen. The day we had waited for our whole lives would be very challenging with this device, which Elise had to have strapped to her leg everywhere she went. Even so, God used this period of hardship and pain during our engagement to grow and mature us in our relationship with him and in our love and commitment to each other. In her typical humor, I remember Elise saying to me several days before the wedding, "We have a ring bearer. Now we just need to find a catheter bearer for the ceremony." Thankfully, the doctors were able to remove the catheter just a few days before we walked down the aisle. I was one happy man!

Suffering Produces Growth

Often, Christians see suffering as an unwanted obstacle to their spiritual growth in Christ. Or perhaps they believe suffering comes upon them as punishment for some wrong they have done. Despite the suffering, hardship and struggles we experienced during our engagement, we both now clearly see how God brought us closer to Him and each other through that experience.

Some see suffering as meaningless and believe that nothing beneficial can come from it. However, God often uses these times more than any other to grow and mature us in our spiritual journey of following Jesus. Typically, we in the West want a "happy" Christianity that is free of all suffering and pain. Our prayers are filled with this kind of thinking: "Lord, keep us safe," "Lord, make us prosperous," "Lord, make us happy." As I am in different churches, I hear these kinds of prayers often. I always find myself thinking, "These are nice prayers, but are they really biblical?"

I once heard Dr. Tony Campolo relate his experience of asking parents in Japan what they wanted for their children. They responded by saying, "We want our children to be successful." He later asked Italian parents the same question, and they responded, "We want our children to be good." But when he asks American parents what they want for their children, they usually respond with "We want them to be happy and safe."

(I, too, have asked this question of people from different cultures around the world. When I ask people from India, they say they want their children to be "noble." When I ask Koreans, they say, "Diligent." When I ask Thai people, they say, "Hard workers.")

If we're honest about our desires, we realize that many of us in the West want the "good life" for our children and for ourselves—a life free from all pain, hurt and suffering. However, that sort of life is not reality and no one will ever be able to find it this side of heaven. Just as you can't avoid getting wet if you jump in the ocean, so you cannot live without suffering and pain.

When did Jesus ever promise happiness or safety for those who chose to follow him? I have had people say to me, "I am really suffering through this situation and I just don't understand why God allowed it to happen. I don't see any way this experience can help me learn or grow." In reality, the opposite is true. Hardship is one of the most effective tools God uses to help us grow and mature into the kind of people He wants us to be.

Throughout Scripture, we see how God uses suffering to build us, transform us and grow us into Christlikeness. As the Apostle Peter wrote to the Christians of his day, so he writes to us, "Dear friends, do not be surprised at the painful trial you are suffering, as though something strange were happening to you. But rejoice that you participate in the sufferings of Christ, so that you may be overjoyed when his glory is revealed."[1]

Whatever circumstance causes pain in our lives, God wants us to embrace that pain and let him use it to grow us in our faith, rather than run from it or pretend it doesn't exist.

Do you know people who are really good at giving you the "right" answer rather than the "real" answer? Often we ask others, "How are you?" and the response is as superficial as it is automatic. "Fine. Just fine." To ignore your pain or to live in denial of it is not good. We should be honest with our pain, but also use discernment and wisdom in choosing with whom we share our struggles. I have often seen people only get more injured after being vulnerable or overly honest with someone they did not know well or with someone who was not mature enough to genuinely listen to their struggle.

Understanding Paradox in Scripture

A paradox is a statement that seems on the surface to be nonsensical, but is in fact true. You will find many paradoxes throughout Scripture, and all of them, though seeming to be self-contradicting, are actually true to the core. Life is filled with mystery, paradox and parable. It is not all meant to fit into nicely organized categories and solutions. Scientists tell us that we use less than 10 percent of our brains to understand the basic facts of our world—

things like $2 + 2 = 4$ and water boils at 100 degrees Centigrade. The other 90 percent of our brain, scientists say, is wrapped in mystery. Perhaps that dominant portion of our brains is reserved for trying to understand the more mysterious aspects of life.

When you read the Bible you will soon find that paradox is everywhere. For example, the Scripture tells us that if you want to live, you must first die. "I have been crucified with Christ and I no longer live, but Christ lives in me. The life I live in the body, I live by faith in the Son of God, who loved me and gave himself for me."[2] Jesus also says that if you really want to find your life, you must loose it first (Matthew 16:25). Christ also says if you want to be exalted, you must humble yourself (Matthew 23:12). In our spiritual journeys, often the way up is to first go down.

Death Leads to Life and Growth

What will bring about the continued growth of the church in the world? How will the church expand in regions of the world where it does not yet exist? Surely, it will be when the people of God respond around the world and choose to live among ethnic groups that have very little or no Christian witness. As Paul's ambition was "to preach the gospel where Christ was not known, so that I would not be building on someone else's foundation,"[3] so should ours be.

However, it will not be through our strategy or our clever ideas that the world is won, but through our blood and the blood of our sons and daughters. The early church father, Tertullian said, "The Blood of the Martyrs is the seed of the church." This means that wherever the blood of Christians has been shed, the church has grown. History proves this fact. Yes, strategy, wisdom and planning are crucial, but they cannot replace the deeper reality: the very blood of people's lives will prepare the soil for people to hear and believe the Gospel.

One of the first missionaries to Korea was Robert J. Thomas. He was ordained on June 4, 1863 at a little church in Hanover, Wales. He and his wife left in July, sent by the London Missionary Society and soon arrived at Shanghai, China. His wife died not long after their arrival. In 1866, having evangelized for a few months in Korea and studied the language, Thomas rode the American ship, General Sherman, along the Taedong River (where the capital of North Korea is today). The Sherman became grounded on a sandbar. The Korean soldiers on shore were suspicious and scared. They boarded the ship waving long knives. When Thomas saw he was going to be killed, he held out the Korean Bible to them saying, "Jesus, Jesus." They cut off his head. Twenty-five years after Thomas' death, someone discovered a little guest house in that same area with some strange wallpaper. The paper had Korean characters printed on it. The owner of the house explained he had pasted the pages of this book on the wall to preserve the writing.

Not only the owner, but many of the guests who stayed "read the walls." This was the Bible that Thomas had given to his murderers. Today, it is said that South Korea is more than 30 percent Christian. Some would even estimate this percentage to be higher. I believe it was the heart and boldness of Robert Thomas that paved the way for others to carry the Gospel to Korea. He was not afraid to give his life so others would have a chance to hear the Gospel of Jesus Christ.

I have preached in Korea several times. I always ask Korean pastors what caused the amazing growth of the church in South Korea over the past 50 years. The answer is always the same, "Prayer and the blood of the missionaries who brought the Gospel to us."

Jesus said, "I tell you the truth, unless a kernel of wheat falls to the ground and dies, it remains only a single seed. But if it dies, it produces many seeds." (John 12:24) Jesus was talking about His own death in this passage, illustrating that His death was necessary to establish His Kingdom. His disciples thought He was going to establish an earthly kingdom, but it was only through the death of Jesus that the will of God would be done.

I believe the reason many areas of the world have very few followers of Jesus is because we are not willing to go, at any cost, and shed our own blood or allow the blood of our children to be shed for Christ's sake. The well known Christian martyr, Jim Elliott, wrote, "He is no fool to give up what he cannot keep, in order to gain what he cannot loose."[4]

Persecution in the First Century Church

Acts 1:8 is a famous verse used to explain the purpose of the church, both locally and globally. After His resurrection, Jesus said to His disciples, "But you will receive power when the Holy Spirit comes on you; and you will be my witnesses in Jerusalem, and in all Judea and Samaria, and to the ends of the earth."

The Greek word used for witness is *martus* (mar'-toos).[5] The word "martyr" is derived from this Greek word.

The 1st Century disciples all faced this reality. According to history and the classic book, *Fox's Book of Martyrs*, all of Jesus' apostles except John faced a martyr's death—along with hundreds of other 1st Century believers. This is said to be one of the greatest evidences of the resurrection of Jesus. If Jesus had not been raised from the dead, why would all these followers of Jesus so willingly lay down their lives for Him?

Stephen, whose story is recorded in the book of Acts, was the first martyr after Jesus. He was cast out of the city and stoned to death. His death marked the beginning of a great persecution that arose against all who professed their belief in Christ as the Messiah. As Luke described it, "...there was a great persecution against the church which was at Jerusalem;" and "...they were all scattered abroad throughout the regions of Judea and Samaria, except the apostles."[6] About 2,000 Christians, including Nicanor, one of the seven deacons, suffered martyrdom during the persecution that arose after Stephen's murder.

James was the elder brother of John and a relative of Jesus. His death took place 10 years after Stephen's. *Fox's Book of Martyrs* gives this account:

"The account given us by an eminent primitive writer, Clemens Alexandrinus, ought not to be overlooked; that, as James was led to the place of martyrdom, his accuser was brought to repent of his conduct by the apostle's extraordinary courage and undauntedness. He fell down at his feet to request his pardon, professing himself a Christian and resolving that James should not receive the crown of martyrdom alone. Hence they were both beheaded at the same time. Thus did the first apostolic martyr cheerfully and resolutely receive that cup, which he had told our Savior he was ready to drink. Timon and Parmenas suffered martyrdom about the same time; the one at Philippi, and the other in Macedonia. These events took place A.D. 44."

Philip was scourged, thrown into prison and crucified in A.D. 54.

Matthew suffered martyrdom by being slain with a halberd in the city of Nadabah in A.D. 60.

James, who was 94 at the time of his martyrdom, was beaten and stoned by the Jews; and finally had his brains dashed out with a fuller's club.

Matthias, of whom less is known than of most of the other disciples, was elected to fill the vacant place of Judas. He was stoned at Jerusalem and then beheaded.

Andrew was the brother of Peter. He preached the Gospel to many Asiatic nations; but upon his arrival at Edessa he was taken and crucified on a cross.

Mark was dragged to pieces by the people of Alexandria.

Peter was condemned to death and crucified in Rome. He was crucified upside down at his own request, because he was (he said) unworthy to be crucified in the same manner as the Lord.

Paul, after his great missionary journeys in preaching the Gospel of Christ, fell under persecution by Nero. The Roman emperor had Paul taken out of the city and killed with a sword.

Jude, the brother of James, was commonly called Thaddeus. He was crucified at Edessa in A.D. 72.

Bartholomew was cruelly beaten and then crucified.

Thomas preached the Gospel in India. His message inciting the rage of the pagan priests, and he was martyred by being thrust through with a spear.

Luke, the author of the Gospel that goes under his name, traveled with Paul through various countries, and is said to have been hanged on an olive tree by the idolatrous priests of Greece.

Simon preached the Gospel in Mauritania, Africa, and finally in Britain where he was crucified in A.D. 74.

Barnabas' death is supposed to have taken place about A.D. 73.

John, the "beloved disciple," was cast into a cauldron of boiling oil. He escaped by miracle, without injury. Afterward, Domitian banished him to the Isle of Patmos, where he wrote the Book of Revelation. Nerva, successor of Domitian, recalled him. He was the only apostle who escaped a violent death.

Global Persecution Today

Christian persecution did not end in the 1st Century, of course. It has continued to impact the church throughout the centuries—from the time of the first disciples right up to the present today. Missiologists estimate that in the 20th Century alone more Christians were martyred for their faith than in all the previous centuries combined.[7] It is important to understand that the problem that lies before us throughout the world today is nothing new. In more than 60 countries, according to an official U.S. State Department report, Christians face the reality of massacre, rape, torture, mutilation, family division, harassment, imprisonment, slavery and discrimination in education and employment.[8] According to the organization, The International Day for Prayer for the Persecuted Church (www.persecutedchurch.org), about 200 million Christians around the world face overt persecution, and another 350 million face various forms of discrimination and restrictions.

While visiting pastors from Sudan in the refugee camps in Uganda, I was so stunned to discover that every one of them had a unique story of religious persecution to share. Each had suffered injustice at the hands of others because of their faith in Christ or their leadership role in the church. The stories ranged from having their churches burned to having a finger chopped off. One man told me the horrific tale of his church members being thrown into an empty water well and having gasoline poured over them. They were set on fire and he was forced to watch them burn to death.

Another man told of the time a revolver had been put to his head with just one bullet in the chamber. The trigger was pulled, and he was forced to endure the mental torture of not knowing if it would go off. Through these men, there was such calm and forgiveness evident in their hearts. They all shared their desire to go back and share the love and forgiveness of Jesus with their oppressors. It was an experience I will never forget. I am certain many crowns await these men in heaven.

Here's a quick overview of just some of the "hot spot" regions of the world where persecution is especially strong today:

In **Nepal** there is still an anti-conversion law in the constitution. You can face seven years in prison if you convert to Christianity.

In parts of **India**, Hindu nationalism rises against both Christians and Muslims. Hindu zealots often beat those of other faiths, publicly ridicule them and prevent them from getting jobs.

In **Egypt**, Muslim attacks against Coptic Christians are common and are not being effectively countered by the government. The government, in fact, is often complicit in the persecution, as it frequently restricts expansion and even repair of Christian facilities by withholding building permits.

In **Iran** converting from Islam to another faith is a criminal offense. Christians are routinely threatened, arrested, imprisoned and tortured because of their faith.

In **Nigeria**, a religiously divided country, Christians are located primarily in the south; while the north is largely Muslim. The government appears to be conducting a campaign to eradicate all evidence of

Christianity in the northern part of the country. Church burning is common.

In **North Korea,** the entire country is suffering from a devastating famine; starvation and near starvation is common. Even with this overshadowing struggle, however, Christians are still regularly persecuted and imprisoned for their belief.

In **Pakistan,** Christians have frequently been the target of trumped up charges of blasphemy. They are often the target of violent mobs of fundamentalist Muslims. A high court judge who had the courage to acquit Christians in one blasphemy case was subsequently assassinated.

In **Saudi Arabia** all Christian worship is forbidden—even within the U.S. embassy. Saudi Muslim citizens who convert to Christianity are subject to the death penalty.

In **Vietnam,** the government requires all religious groups to register. But since the civil war ended in the mid 1970s, no protestant group has been granted official recognition. The government rigidly controls the Catholic Church by placing official restrictions on the number of students permitted in seminaries, restricting the number of ordinations allowed by law, and several other similar anti-Christian regulations.

The Biblical Perspective on Persecution

In order to truly understand why persecution against Christians exists in the world today and how we should respond it, it is vital to examine this important theme from a biblical perspective. Here are a few key Scriptures you can use to begin your own exploration of this important topic. But this list is by no means exhaustive. As you study the Word, watch for other verses that address the issue of suffering for your faith.

The Bible says, "Everyone who wants to live a godly life in Christ Jesus will be persecuted."[9] However, we should not let this news discourage you from following Jesus with your whole heart because the Bible also speaks clearly of the heavenly rewards awaiting us for the suffering we endure in this life. "Blessed is the man who perseveres under trial because when he has stood the test, he will receive the crown of life God has promised to those who love him."[10]

The Bible also lists several benefits of suffering that come to us on this side of heaven. One of the most important of these is spiritual maturity: "Consider it pure joy, my brothers, whenever you face trials of many kinds because you know that the testing of your faith develops perseverance. Perseverance must finish its work so you may be mature and complete, not lacking anything."[11]

We can also take comfort in knowing God will bring justice to those who persecute Christians when Jesus returns. "All this is evidence that God's judgment is right and as a result you will be counted worthy of the kingdom of God, for which you are suffering. God is just: He will pay back trouble to those who trouble you."[12]

We should not fear death as followers of Jesus. Perhaps it is human and natural to fear the manner in which we will die or the pain we may suffer that leads us to death, but death for the Christian is merely the doorway into heaven and the presence of God. It is not the end or something to be confused about.

I am amazed how many Christians I talk to fear death. The Bible says, "Now we know that if the earthly tent we live in is destroyed, we have a building from God, an eternal house in heaven, not built by human hands. Meanwhile we groan, longing to be clothed with our heavenly dwelling because when we are clothed, we will not be found naked. For while we are in this tent, we groan and are burdened because we do not wish to be unclothed but to be clothed with our heavenly dwelling, so that what is mortal may be swallowed up by life. We live by faith, not by sight. We are confident, I say, and would prefer to be away from the body and at home with the Lord. So we make it our goal to please him, whether we are at home in the body or away from it."[13]

God uses persecution and trials for His purposes. His purpose is that all people on earth will worship Him and know Him through faith in Jesus Christ. Persecution solidifies within our hearts a genuine faith that glorifies Jesus Christ. The Bible says, "These [sufferings] have come so that your faith—of greater worth than gold, which perishes even though refined by fire—may be proved genuine and may result in praise, glory and honor when Jesus Christ is revealed."[14]

Persecution also reveals Jesus Christ in us. The Bible says, "But we have this treasure in jars of clay to show that this all-surpassing power is from God and not from us. We are hard pressed on every side, but not crushed; perplexed, but not in despair; persecuted, but not abandoned; struck down, but not destroyed. We always carry around in our body the death of Jesus, so that the life of Jesus may also be revealed in our body. For we who are alive are always being given over to death for Jesus' sake, so that His life may be revealed in our mortal body."[15]

Suffering encourages others to be more courageous in their testimony. When you see others being persecuted for their faith in Jesus Christ, their example of faith inspires you to become more bold and confident in sharing your own faith in Christ. The Bible says, "Now I want you to know, brothers, that what has happened to me has really served to advance the gospel. As a result, it has become clear throughout the whole palace guard and to everyone else that I am in chains for Christ. Because of my chains, most of the brothers in the Lord have been encouraged to speak the word of God more courageously and fearlessly."[16]

Finally, persecution does something amazing in that it actually spreads the Gospel to other places. The Book of Acts records, "On that day a great persecution broke out against the church at Jerusalem, and all except the apostles were scattered throughout Judea and Samaria."[17]

"Those who had been scattered preached the Word wherever they went. Philip went down to a city in Samaria and proclaimed the Christ there."[18]

The Biblical Response to Persecution

There are numerous examples in the Bible to help us understand how we should respond to persecution:

• **We should remember the persecuted as if we ourselves were suffering.** "Remember those in prison as if you were their fellow prisoners, and those who are mistreated as if you yourselves were suffering."[19]

• **We should stand side by side with the persecuted believers around the world, and even accept personal loss in order to support them**. "Remember those earlier days after you had received the light, when you stood your ground in a great contest in the face of suffering. Sometimes you were publicly exposed to insult and persecution; at other times you stood side by side with those who were so treated. You sympathized with those in prison and joyfully accepted the confiscation of your property, because you knew that you yourselves had better and lasting possessions."[20]

• **We should encourage other Christians with the stories of faith and endurance we hear about.** Paul wrote, "Therefore, among God's churches we boast about your perseverance and faith in all the persecutions and trials you are enduring."[21] Paul boasted to other Christians about the persecution that the believers in Thessalonica endured as they followed Jesus Christ.

• **We should take action to rescue the persecuted.** "Rescue those being led away to death; hold back those staggering toward slaughter.[22] Many times we have the tendency to respond to those who are persecuted in other lands solely by praying for them. While this is good, the Bible says we should show as much concern for the persecuted "over there" as we would if they lived in our own community. We are all a part of the same family. "So that there should be no division in the body, but that its parts should have equal concern for each other. If one part suffers, every part suffers with it; if one part is honored, every part rejoices with it."[23]

• **We should love and pray for the ones who are persecuting believers.** This is much easier said than done. Jesus said, "You have heard that it was said, 'Love your neighbor and hate your enemy.' But I tell you: Love your enemies and pray for those who persecute you."[24] As you pray for those who persecute the church, remember who the true enemy is. Paul tells us in the book of Ephesians, "For our struggle is not against flesh and blood, but against the rulers, against the authorities, against the powers of this dark world and against the spiritual forces of evil in the heavenly realms. Therefore, put on the full armor of God, so that when the day of evil comes, you may be able to stand your ground, and after you have done everything, to stand."[25]

Sudan is a region in the world where Christians have been killed for their faith and ministry to Jesus. It is also a place where the church has grown through this persecution. Joseph Oloya Hakim is a ServLife missionary in Africa. He is from Sudan and has personally witnessed great atrocities against Christians, many of whom have been put to death for their faith. Reflecting on the reality of persecution and its true source, he writes, "We here are in exile from our mother land, Sudan. We persevere and strive for maturity wherever we live. I believe effective Christian maturity is not so much a goal to be achieved, but rather a lifestyle to be developed. From all points on the compass, all along the line of battle, in the vanguard and in the rear, at dawn of the day and in the midnight hour, Satan hinders us.

"If we toil in the fields, he seeks to break the ploughshares; if we build the walls, he labors to cast down the stones, if we serve God in sufferings and in conflicts—everywhere, Satan hinders us. He hinders our coming to Christ Jesus; he endeavors to hinder the completeness of our personal character. Yet, I am not alarmed because Satan hinders us, for it is a proof we are doing God's work and in His strength, we shall win the victory and triumph over our adversary. God bless you and may He use you to be a light to all the world."

Satan does not want the Church to be fueled with a fearless passion and a desire to see God known and worshiped on every shore and among every tribe. He does all he can to keep the Church consumed with her own building projects, her own comfort and her own entertainment. Remember who our enemy is.

• Finally, no matter what we endure for the sake of the Gospel, we should always rejoice over their steadfast love of God. "Therefore, brothers, in all our distress and persecution we were encouraged about you because of your faith. For now we really live, since you are standing firm in the Lord. How can we thank God enough for you in return for all the joy we have in the presence of our God because of you? Night and day we pray most earnestly that we may see you again and supply what is lacking in your faith."[26]

A Few Stories of Modern Day Persecution

At 9 p.m. on Monday, January 12, 1992 gunmen burst into a churchyard in Isfara, north of Tajikistan, and fired several rounds through a window at Sergei, a local pastor as he knelt in prayer. On hearing the gunfire, his wife, Tamara rushed to her husband's side, but he was already dead. He was shot 13 times with a Kalashnikov assault rifle. A local newspaper only a week before had attacked Sergei for his missionary work in this staunchly Muslim region.

The hard line Islamic Revival Party garnered a large majority of the local vote in recent elections, despite central government attempts to curb the growth of Islamic extremism. Women often wear the veil in villages. And alcohol is taboo; indeed, shops stocking it have sometimes been burned down. When Sergei began handing out Christian literature, the act aroused considerable local anger.[27]

While ministering in Cambodia a few years ago, I hear a remarkable story from a local Cambodian Christian leader. During the late 1970s, a cruel dictator, Pol Pot rose to power and began a genocide in the slaughter of people within the country. The atrocity later became known as the "Killing Fields." During this time, a pastor named Sujek was thrown in jail for his faith in Jesus Christ and for preaching the Gospel.

After being in prison for several years, Sujek got very discouraged and began doubting his relationship with Jesus and his calling to preach the Gospel to his own people. *I cannot go on,* he thought. *God must have given up on me.* One day he was instructed to clean the outside toilets. These toilets were merely holes dug into of the ground. As he began to clean them, he noticed paper that had been used as toilet paper and thrown onto the grass. He quickly noticed that there was writing on the paper and put it in his pocket. That night, he opened the paper and cleaned off the human excrement and read the words under a candle: "For I am convinced that neither death nor life, neither angels nor demons, neither the present nor the future, nor any powers, neither height nor depth, nor anything else in all creation, will be able to separate us from the love of God that is in Christ Jesus our Lord."[28]

He realized that the prison guards had destroyed the Bibles and used them as toilet paper. The next day he went to the prison guards and requested, "Can I volunteer to go clean the toilet again today?" They were shocked to hear him make this request and granted their permission. As the days turned into weeks and the weeks turned into months, he ended up collecting the entire book of Romans. He was later freed and escaped Cambodia.

Sujek is now back in Cambodia preaching the Gospel of Jesus Christ.

Udaya runs our mission's children home in Kathmandu, Nepal. In 2001, Udaya was sent to prison for over 21 days for conducting a Bible study among university students whose parents were complaining because their children were interested in Jesus. "I greatly enjoyed being in custody," explains Udaya. "I was able to share with many people about Jesus Christ."

I wonder if student workers in the West would still do student ministry if they faced the possibility of going to jail?

Some friends in the Middle East run a book shop that is used to help do ministry and provide Christian books throughout the region. During one of my visits, I learned that they had just had their book shop set on fire by the local militant Muslim community. Letters, threatening the lives of the Arab followers of Jesus, were shown to me. Seeing the courage and commitment of these Arab Christians in the midst of such opposition is something that will always inspire and motivate me to love and serve Jesus more fully.

The director of our ministry in India, Albert, shares many experiences of being personally assaulted for his faith. On one occasion while preaching the Gospel in northern India, militant Hindus threw stones at him and his team, shouting, "Stop speaking of this God."

Albert and his team continued to proclaim the Gospel despite being hit by these stones. "I will never stop preaching and proclaiming about the love of God," Albert says with a grin. "They can kill me. I do not care. I would love to meet Jesus while preaching the Gospel!"

Responding to Persecution through the Lens of Community

We do not look down on those who are persecuted for their faith, for that would lead us to pride. We also do not put them up on a pedestal, for that would lead to idolatry. Instead, we need to look upon our persecuted brothers and sisters around the world as family and a part of our community of faith. Hebrews 13:3 tells us, "Remember those in prison and those who are suffering as if you, yourself were suffering."

An early church mystic said, "We were created in the image of the laughter of the Trinity!" This means we were created in the image of community: The Father, Son and Holy Spirit. We must have community to fully know what a journey of faith in Christ is.

Of course, that community of faith begins in a local context—through a local church. But we must also come to know community in an historical context so we can better understand how and why we exist as the Church today and about the men and women who lived and served before us. Finally, we must have community globally.

We have the privilege to be in community with our brothers and sisters around the world. It is not an obligation, but a true honor. If we want to understand the ways of God, discern the words of Jesus and unlock the mysteries of the Kingdom, then we must be in community with our persecuted brothers and sisters around the world. We must be in community with those we have never known on American soil and yet who suffer degrees of injustice.

Paul gives the metaphor of the body of Christ as being like the human body. He writes, "...so that there should be no division in the body, but that its parts should have equal concern for each other. If one part suffers, every part suffers with it; if one part is honored, every part rejoices with it."[29]

A Few Practical Suggestions on How to Respond

As many in the world suffer for their faith and ministry in Christ, we must care. Here are a few practical suggestions for living out that compassion in practical ways:

• **Get informed on where persecution exists in the world.** Subscribe to email lists, purchase books or talk to your missionary friends to educate yourself on where persecution is greatest today. Here are a few good places to start:

- Christian Freedom International (www.christianfreedom.org)
- Human Rights Watch (www.hrw.org)
- Amnesty International (www.amnesty.org)
- Christian Solidarity Worldwide (www.cswusa.com)
- Voice of the Martyrs International (www.persecution.net)
- Open Doors with Brother Andrew (www.opendoorsusa.org)

• **Write your political leaders, both state and national, and inform them of your concern for the countries that persecute Christians.** You can contact your federal representative and senator via email by going to www.house.gov and www.senate.gov, respectively. In a similar way, you can contact your state officials by visiting your state's official website (www.[your state].gov).

• **Pray for those who are persecuted.** Pray that Jesus will appear before the persecutors as he did to Saul on the road to Damascus. Prayer is vital and a great way to organize your small group or your whole church to support those who are being persecuted in the world today for their faith in Jesus Christ.

• **Write letters of encouragement to Christians who are in prison for their faith around the world.** Visit www.prisoneralert.com for more information.

Questions for Personal Reflection or Small Group Study:

1. Think back to a time in your life when you experienced a season of suffering. What did you learn from that experience? Did it bring you closer to God? Why or why not?

2. Which paradox of the Gospel is the most difficult for you to understand? What could you do to understand it better?

3. Think back to a time you heard a story of someone being persecuted for his or her faith. How did it impact you?

4. Do you agree with the idea that people must die for Jesus Christ in various regions of the world in order for the church to grow? Why or why not?

5. Which Scriptures in this chapter spoke to you the most? How did they impact you?

Notes

1. 1 Peter 4:12-13
2. Galatians 2:20
3. Romans 15:20-21
4. Elisabeth Elliot, *In The Shadow of the Almighty* (Harper and Row, 1958)
5. *Biblesoft's New Exhaustive Strong's Numbers and Concordance with Expanded Greek-Hebrew Dictionary* (Biblesoft and International Bible Translators, Inc., 1994)
6. Acts 8:1
7. *World Christian Encyclopedia* (Two Volumes), edited by D.B. Barrett, G.T. Kurian and T.M. Johnson (Oxford University Press, 2001)
8. www.state.gov
9. 2 Timothy 3:12
10. James 1:12
11. James 1:2-5
12. 2 Thessalonians 1:5-7
13. 2 Corinthians 5:1-9
14. 1 Peter 1:7-8
15. 2 Corinthians 4:7-11
16. Philippians 1:12-14
17. Acts 8:1
18. Acts 8:4-5
19. Hebrews 13:2-3
20. Hebrews 10:32-34
21. 2 Thessalonians 1:4
22. Proverbs 24:11
23. 1 Corinthians 12:25-26
24. Matthew 5:43-45
25. Ephesians 6:12-13
26. 1 Thessalonians 3:7-10
27. The Barnabas Fund
28. Romans 8:38-39
29. 1 Corinthians 12:25-26

CHAPTER
8

A God of Justice

"Injustice anywhere affects justice everywhere."
—*Dr. Martin Luther King*

"Speak up for those who cannot speak for themselves, for the rights of all who are destitute. Speak up and judge fairly; defend the rights of the poor and needy."
—Proverbs 31:8-9

Nuraj and Ramesh were normal Indian boys who were extremely poor and lived in a rural village. Their home was like most in their small village—made of mud and grass. One day, their world came crashing in on them when their father died and they were subsequently abandoned by their mother. They were sold by distant relatives to the local land lord because of a debt. Their days as five- and seven-year-old boys were no longer spent playing with other children on the playground or being educated in school. Their days were long and hot. Without adequate food, they sat on stones for 12 hours each day. They held hammers in their hands, breaking rocks into small stones. They did this seven days a week, never getting even a day to rest.

Thousands of children in India alone are in some sort of bonded labor like Nuraj and Ramesh. But unlike most of their peers, their story has a happier ending.

A pastor in their village heard of these boys and was determined to get cared for in an appropriate way. Through the pastor's efforts, the boys were freed and brought to ServLife's ministry center in India in 1997. Thus, an orphanage was established.

Nuraj and Ramesh are now about 13 and 15 years old, as I write this. When you ask them what they want to be when they leave ServLife Children's Home, they say, "I want to be a pastor when I grow up like daddy (referring to Albert, the director of ServLife India) and go back to my home village and tell people about Jesus."

When you read the story of these brothers, are there not emotions that stir up within you? Do you not say to yourself, "How can anyone think of doing something like this to a child?"

Well, the reality is that what happened to these boys goes on every day all around the world—effectively destroying the lives and hopes of thousands upon thousands of innocent children. It is unjust and wrong.

Analysis Leads to Paralysis

I have found time and time again from traveling through the world and ministering in different places that there is a cold apathy among many Christians when it comes to issues of injustice going on around the world. There is concern, but often that concern leads nowhere. People's analytical thinking often leaves them feeling helpless and paralyzed. This is exactly what the devil wants—unresponsive and immobile Christians.

We see injustice on television. We read in missionary newsletters or hear reports at our churches, and we are just overwhelmed at the reality of wrong things done to the innocent. "How can I help?" you may ask. Or you may also say, "There is just too much suffering. I cannot possibly do anything to make a difference."

However, if we are honest, deep inside our hearts something wells up within us and wants to take action. Too often, however, we do not know what to do.

Gary Haugen, founder of the International Justice Mission, says that when Christians are confronted with the injustices of the world, it is as if our hearts become like deer frozen in the headlights of a car. The information that should provoke us to action does the exact opposite. The effect is similar to what happens when you eat a meal that is supposed to provide energy for your body, but instead makes you feel like lying down and taking a nap.[1]

Solomon wrote, "Again I looked and saw all the oppression that was taking place under the sun: I saw the tears of the oppressed—and they have no comforter; power was on the side of their oppressors—and they have no comforter."[2] Indeed, Solomon's reaction rings true for anyone who gazes out into a troubled world filled with so much pain, injustice and human suffering. What can we do? Perhaps we cannot change the whole world, but we can change the world one life at a time through the power of Christ, who lives in us and works through us. I believe many of you want to make a difference—or you would not be reading this.

In my view, there are three primary reasons why we should respond to issues of injustice around the world:

• **We know God.** Eternal life is knowing God now—it isn't merely going to heaven when we die. Jesus said, "Now this is eternal life: that they may know you, the only true God, and Jesus Christ, whom you have sent."[3] Perhaps you have thought that following Jesus is only a means to get a ticket into heaven and has nothing to do with your life on earth. That could not be farther from the truth. As we come to know the God of the Bible, we clearly see His heart and passion for justice throughout His Word. One of the common problems for many of us who follow Jesus Christ is that we are not often reminded of the Scriptures that speak on the theme of justice. And yet, the Scriptures are filled with the theme. Allow me to remind you.

The Bible says, "The Lord loves righteousness and justice; the earth is full of his unfailing love."[4] God said to Jeremiah, "'But let him who boasts boast about this: that he understands and knows me, that I am the Lord, who exercises kindness, justice and righteousness on earth, for in these I delight,' declares the Lord."[5] The Psalmist said, "For the Lord is righteous, he loves justice; upright men will see his face."[6] God said to Isaiah, "For I, the Lord, love justice; I hate robbery and iniquity. In my faithfulness I will reward them and make an everlasting covenant with them."[7] The Bible even tells us specifically what it means to seek justice, "Learn to do right! Seek justice, encourage the oppressed. Defend the cause of the fatherless, plead the case of the widow."[8]

In responding to issues of injustice, we must not merely observe but act. Jesus modeled equality and empowerment for the voiceless. Remember the woman at the well (John 4) and the little children who sat on Jesus' lap (Mark 10)? In both of these stories, Jesus modeled going against the religious viewpoint of the day. In Jesus' day, it was far out of the social norm for men to talk to a Samaritan woman or to interact with children in the street. The very act of doing this communicated that we are all equal before God and should be treated fairly and with justice

God clearly tells us what our response to injustice should be. The Bible says, "He has showed you, O man, what is good. And what does the LORD require of you? To act justly and to love mercy and to walk humbly with your God."[9]

• **We are citizens of the Kingdom of God.** I have to ask myself, "Why is so much of the church silent on the issue of injustice?" Perhaps it is because of the way we preach the Gospel of Jesus Christ. Much of the church has reduced the Gospel as solely the Good News that gets people into heaven and does nothing more for us on earth. Indeed, the Gospel gives us peace when we face death, since Jesus promised a home for us in heaven, but the Gospel is far more than that. The power of the Gospel of Jesus Christ is not limited to our "eternal destiny," but impacts every aspect of a person's life in the here and now.

Jesus' primary theme in teachings was "The Kingdom of God." Now, I am fully aware of the many schools of thought on what the Kingdom of God is and the different interpretations on when this Kingdom is supposed to come to reality. However, no one can argue that Jesus spoke on this theme more than any other in the New Testament. His parables were mostly teachings on life in this "Kingdom." He said the Kingdom is not out there somewhere, but is inside you (Luke 17:21). He also prayed, "Your Kingdom come and your will be done on earth as it is in Heaven."[10]

In God's Kingdom there will be no expressions of injustice; therefore, we should strive as Christians on this side of heaven to see justice exercised on the earth. Most would agree as well that the basic idea of God's

Kingdom is the reign and rule of God. When justice is achieved for the fatherless, the oppressed, the widow and the poor in the name of Christ, God's Kingdom is present, and God himself is Honored and glorified.

  • **We are agents of hope in a world of sin.** In Genesis 3, Adam and Eve choose sin and we witnessed what has come to be known as The Fall. Ever since that day, people in our world have been born into sin and are separated from God. We now live in a world where the wickedness of people's hearts leads them to do things that are incomprehensible. As a result, billions of people face poverty and millions of others are held as victims of people's greed, lust, power and desire for control.

Yet, in the midst of the evil that pervades our world, we are the body and bride of Christ. We are here to offer our hands as Jesus did when He was on the earth to touch people with acts of kindness and compassion. We, as the Church, are the feet of Jesus to walk to where people are hurting and suffering and to offer them the hope that is in God. We are the ears of Jesus to listen to those who suffer and to be a friend to them, not trying to push our agenda, but simply to love and listen. We are the eyes of Jesus, always looking for the despised and rejected, that we might go and encourage them.

It has been said that the Church of Jesus Christ is the sole hope of the world. I would argue that it is not the Church but Jesus Christ Himself and His Kingdom that is the hope for the world—and it is He and His Kingdom we are called to proclaim. A person can live 40 days without food, four days without water, four minutes without air, but no one can live even four seconds without hope. Hope is a powerful reality for everyone who breathes. No matter the culture you live in, the desperate need for hope is common to all.

We experience different degrees of hope throughout our lives. For example, there are plenty of "everyday hopes" we all share—the hope of finding a good place to park when we go the airport or the hope of not catching the flu. We also hold bigger hopes for our children to succeed and grow healthy. And yet we have even bigger hopes that our lives will actually have meaning and make a difference in the world. In many of the cultures I have visited, people's hopes and dreams have been crushed because of economic or other forms of injustice. However, I have also witnessed many people in these oppressed regions of the world possesing an astounding, contagious hope—a hope that stems directly from their faith in Jesus Christ. As the Bible says, "We have this hope as an anchor for the soul, firm and secure."[11]

The South African missiologist, David Bosch, wrote, "Christian hope is both possession and yearning, repose and activity, arrival and being on the way. Since God's victory is certain, believers can work both patiently and enthusiastically, blending careful planning with urgent obedience, motivated by the patient impatience of the Christian hope."[12]

I am thrilled, as many are, to see so many Christians respond to Bono, the lead singer to the famous rock group U2, as he speaks out on HIV/AIDS' issues in Africa, eliminating the debt of poorer nations, and other issues of injustice. But at the same time, I am saddened that Christians are not equally moved simply by reading God's Word—seeing His heart for the oppressed and hearing His cry against injustice all throughout Scripture. God must look down on events going on in the world today and be saddened that His church is not doing what we can.

These issues are not exclusively Bono's issues, after all. They belong to all of us. At certain meetings I have attended, I have grown tired of hearing people quote this rock star, although I do respect his work on these important issues. But I believe we must hear the Word of God and let it serve as our guide in addressing the injustices in the world today. I believe great opportunities for the Gospel of Jesus Christ will be available if we, as the church, move to action in combating issues of human trafficking, bonded labor, the environment, HIV/AIDS and other issues of justice.

Human Trafficking

Gune is the most beautiful girl you have ever seen. She is 10 years old and has a face of an angel. I remember the first time I saw her I told my wife that if we could adopt her, I would do it. Gune's story, however, is very distressing. She lived in a small village in rural Nepal. Her parents were poor and uneducated. Her father consumed copious amounts of locally-brewed alcohol most every day and took out his misery on Gune and her mother.

"The Hindu gods must be punishing me," he would often say to his family or to himself. "There is no hope." After one especially brutal night of drunkenness and violence toward his family, Gune's mother took a knife and killed her husband. Gune, who was seven years old at the time, watched in horror as the entire macabre scene played out before her eyes. The authorities arrested her mother and threw her into jail, where she remains to this day. A local pastor heard about this story and brought Gune to ServLife's children's home in India where she now lives. At the children's home, she is provided with an education, meals and, most importantly, love. "My favorite part of the movie of Jesus is when they hung Him on the cross because He died for my sins," she explains. Gune often tells me she wants to be a doctor when she grows up, so she can help others just as she has been helped.

Every time I am with Gune, my heart is moved because I think of the life that could have so easily been hers—that of an enslaved prostitute, sleeping with 15 to 20 men a day at a brothel in some big city in India. You see, young girls like Gune very often end up being trafficked into the extensive sex trade industry based in that region of the world. God's Spirit must compel us to come to the aid of all of the "Gunes" of the world who suffer as innocent victims in this depraved industry.

Trafficking human beings is not the same as smuggling them. Human trafficking involves deceiving or coercing someone to move—either within a country or abroad through legal or illegal channels—for the purpose of exploiting him or her. Smuggling, on the other hand, is assisting someone for a fee to cross a border illegally.[13] Human trafficking has become a $9 billion a year global industry and is becoming increasingly entrenched within large organized crime rings.[14]

Some may think that human trafficking is only an issue outside the western world. Think again. It is impacting America. The U.S. State Department estimates that from 18,000 to 20,000 people are trafficked into the U.S. every year.[15] Every year the American government alone spends about $55 million to combat this issue.[16]

Trafficking involves the buying and selling of humans, usually women or children, for economic gain via means of force or deception. In Nepal, where my family has lived and served for a number of years, it is estimated that 200,000 Nepalese girls under age 16 have been trafficked into India as prostitutes.[17] Another Human Rights organization estimates that an addition 6,000 to 7,000 Nepalese girls end up in Indian brothels every year.[18]

According to one expert, at least half of the 100,000 girl prostitutes between the ages of 10 and 14 in Bombay are originally from Nepal and are kept in brothels against their will.[19]

They are girls just like Gune.

This is a horrible reality. Human trafficking affects people of all ages, but the impact on young girls is especially profound—especially since these children cannot speak up for themselves. I believe there are three important ways we can respond to this atrocious injustice:

• **Prevention.** Perhaps the most effective way to stop the trafficking of the innocent is by preventing it from happening in the first place. This is, of course, is much easier said than done. Such prevention would require change on many levels of society—through educating families at the grassroots level, passing stricter laws to combat organized crime, and working with organizations to provide economic development in areas where trafficking is rampant. Providing opportunities for economic development is particularly important. When people have the basic ability to provide for themselves and pay for their children's education, then they will not be so easily enticed by these unsavory "alternative" means of support.

One of the ways children are trafficked is when the children's parents are approached by so called "businessmen" who promise that their child will earn good money in their factory making "whatever" kind of product. They promise the parents that the child will be well cared for and will be able to send money back to them. The uneducated parents agree and send their child to some distant location thinking they are helping both their child and themselves. They do not realize they are sending their child to be beaten and forced into prostitution or hard labor. These parents are typically extremely poor and illiterate. They are deceived by the apparent opportunity to give their child a marketable skill and create a better life for themselves.

Education is also very important and can go a long way in helping communities who may be prone to this sort of predation. This is where I believe God may be calling some of you who are reading this to step in and help. Perhaps you are exceptional in business and have an entrepreneurial spirit, yet you are struggling with what to do with your life. Why waste your skills on simply making the stockholders happy? Give your life to the cause of preventing human trafficking. Right now all around the world, there is great need for people who have the skills to set up and launch "micro-businesses" in areas where human trafficking is rampant.

A micro business in the developing world can be set up for a mere $250 to $500. Examples of micro-businesses in the developing world can range widely. Perhaps it is a small kiosk to sell fruits and vegetables, several goats to start a goat farm, or making bags or other handicrafts. Micro-business loans to local residents can be given with little or no interest, but the return on investment is huge in terms of lives saved. When the loan is paid back, the money can be used again to help others get started.

There are some large organizations and governments that are doing this in very effective ways, but there are also thousands of grassroots organizations, churches and individuals who are making a difference by helping the poor start their own businesses. Our organization alone has helped 200 Sudan refugees, mostly poor widows, start these kinds of businesses. But much more needs to be done. And you can help.

• **Intervention.** Rescuing those who have been coerced into prostitution or forced labor is another way to intervene. However, a follow up plan for placing these victims in homes and ministries is absolutely crucial. In many places in the world, certain groups focus exclusively on rescuing victims from slavery but do nothing to help the victims become productive members of society. For that reason, many times the victims return to their life of slavery, because it's all they know. Of course, this is not always the case and rescuing the innocent from such a system is crucial. But more intentional intervention is needed to help place people in a healthy environment where they can be educated and loved.

One organization that has pioneered this work and does a great job is the International Justice Mission. Gary Haugen, a Harvard Law School graduate, recruits lawyers to help intervene on behalf of women and children who have no voice.

• **Rehabilitation.** In order to rehabilitate the children who fall victim to trafficking, many more orphanages' and children's homes are desperately needed. James says, "Religion that God our Father accepts as pure and faultless is this: to look after orphans and widows in their distress and to keep oneself from being polluted by the world."[20] Even now as you read this, perhaps God is calling you to move to a place in the world where trafficking is happening and start a children's home so you can share the love of Jesus Christ with children who have come out of this situation. What a worthy goal and ambition for one's life! And we would do well to heed this warning from the Lord: "Administer justice every morning; rescue from the hand of his oppressor the one who has been robbed, or my wrath will break out and burn like fire because of the evil you have done—burn with no one to quench it."[21]

For more information on how you can pursue this worthy goal, email me at info@servlife.org.

Modern Day Slavery

Slavery is still alive and well in the world today. According to the United Nations, the word "slavery" today applies to a variety of human rights violations. In addition to traditional slavery and the slave trade, these abuses include the sale of children, child prostitution, child pornography, the exploitation of child labor, the sexual mutilation of female children, the use of children in armed conflicts, debt bondage, the sale of human organs, the exploitation of adult prostitution and certain practices under apartheid.[22]

Here are a few examples of modern day slavery:

• **Bonded labor.** Bonded labor takes place when a family receives an advance payment (sometimes as little as $15) to hand a child over to an employer. Sometimes they are tricked into doing this. In most cases, the child cannot work off the debt, nor can the family raise enough money to buy the child back. The workplace is often structured so that "expenses" or "interest" are deducted from a child's earnings in such amounts that it is almost impossible for a child to repay the debt. In some cases, the labor is generational—that is, a child's grandfather or great-grandfather was promised to an employer many years earlier, with the understanding that each generation would provide the employer with a new worker... often with no pay at all.[23]

Bonded labor impacts at least 20 million people around the world. To repay the debt, they are forced to work long hours, seven days a week, 365 days a year. They receive basic food and shelter as "payment" for their work, but may never pay off the loan. These children, who are typically between 7 and 10 years of age, work 12 to 14 hours a day and are paid less than one-third a typical adult wage.[24] Remember the story of Nuraj and Ramesh?

• **Child labor.** These are children who work in exploitative or dangerous conditions. Tens of millions of children around the world work full time. Child labor, often hard and hazardous, damages health for life, deprives children of education and the normal enjoyment of their early years. Child labor is in great demand because it is cheap, children are naturally easier to discipline than adults, and they too frightened to complain. Their small physique and nimble fingers are seen as assets by unscrupulous employers for certain kinds of work. It often happens that children are given jobs when their parents are sitting at home, unemployed.

• **Early and forced marriage.** This affects women and girls who are married without choice and who are forced into lives of servitude, often accompanied by physical violence.

Early and forced marriage happens on a regular basis among the poor around the world. Within nations around Africa, usually the boy pays a dowry to the woman's family in order to secure a bride. In India, it is the opposite. The girl's family pays a dowry to the boy's family. In many villages, young girls are given to marriage before they even reach puberty.

The Environment

The Bible says, "The earth is the Lord's, and everything in it, the world, and all who live in it."[25] The earth belongs to God. God causes all things to grow on the earth and has given food for humankind. The earth is the gift of God. It is the production of His hand and the fruit of His goodness and love.[26] What makes us think that the earth is *our* property? We are merely stewards and have a responsibility to care for what God has given us. We should be thankful. The Bible says, "For everything

God created is good, and nothing is to be rejected if it is received with thanksgiving."[27]

One Bible Scholar writes, "And because God made the earth and its fullness, all animals, plants and vegetables, there can be nothing in it or them impure or unholy; because all are the creatures of God."[28] The Bible says, "Through him all things were made; without him nothing was made that has been made."[29] And "...for him all things were created: things in heaven and on earth, visible and invisible, whether thrones or powers or rulers or authorities; all things were created by him and for him. He is before all things, and in him all things hold together."[30]

Many Christians think about or talk about the environment and our stewardship of it as Christ followers. And yet the first time God spoke to human beings, He said, "Have babies *and take care of the earth*."[31] We have a responsibility to care for all God has created. However, if you look at our world today, you will see a planet in danger of becoming far from what God originally created. We, as followers of Christ, must be concerned. Problems related to fresh water alone kill thousands of people every day. Pollution causes health issues that are damaging for life. Did you know that half of the forests that originally covered 46 percent of the Earth's land surface are gone? Only one-fifth of the Earth's original forests remain pristine and undisturbed.[32]

Between 10 and 20 percent of all species will be driven to extinction in the next 20 to 50 years. Based on current trends, an estimated 34,000 plant and 5,200 animal species—including one in eight of the world's bird species—face extinction. Almost a quarter of the world's mammal species will face extinction within 30 years. Up to 47 percent of the world's plant species are at risk of extinction. Sixty percent of the world's coral reefs, which contain up to one-fourth of all marine species, could be lost in the next 20 to 40 years.

Hundreds of thousands of sea turtles and marine mammals are entangled and drowned by irresponsible fishing practices every year. More than 20 percent of the world's known 10,000 freshwater fish species have become extinct, been threatened or endangered in recent decades. Sixty percent of the world's important fish stocks are threatened from over fishing. Desertification and land degradation threaten nearly one-quarter of the land surface of the globe.

More than 250 million people are directly affected by desertification, and one billion people are at risk. Global warming is expected to increase the earth's temperature by 3 degrees Centigrade (5.4 degrees Fahrenheit) in the next 100 years, resulting in multiple adverse effects on the environment, including widespread species loss, ecosystem damage, flooding of populated human settlements, and increased natural disasters.[33]

As we understand that God has placed us as stewards of the earth, we should care for it and respond to the problems facing the planet. Here are some practical suggestions of how you can start helping now:

- Recycle in your home and church.
- Start a cell phone drive—250 million used mobile phones are lying around in this country in land fills. Start a cell phone drive and collect old phones. Our mission has done this and has raised over $1,500 for our work around the world.
- Carpool and drive less.
- Make a donation to drill clean water wells in the poor regions of the world. This can be done for just a few hundred dollars. Thousands still die every day from dirty water.

- Get educated on the issues by exploring the Evangelicals for Social Action's website at www.esa-online.org.

Lack of Education

There is an Indian proverb that says, "Educating your daughter is like watering your neighbor's garden." In India, as in many places in the world, the value of educating a girl is not very high. Today, a child in Mozambique can expect to go to school for two to three years, with luck. Meanwhile, a five-year old European or North American child can expect to spend 17 years in formal education.[34]

Today, a decade after the rallying cry of Education for All, there are still 125 million children in the world who never attend school. An additional 150 million children of primary age start school, but drop out before they can read or write. Today, sub-Saharan Africa accounts for one-third of the total out-of-school population. With current trends, that region will account for three-quarters of the total by the year 2015. One in four adults in the developing world—872 million people—is illiterate, and the numbers are growing.[35]

Perhaps you are now realizing the importance of this issue, and you are wondering how you can help. Here is where to start:

- Give up your vacation time; instead, volunteer to teach in a region of the world where teachers are desperately needed.
- Sponsor a child to get an education. There are dozens of child sponsorship organizations. Choose one you like. If you don't know of one, email me at info@servlife.org.
- Collect used books and send them to schools in the world that could use them.

- Give up a year or two and go teach in the world.
- Tutor children who are at risk or volunteer in an after-chool program in your area.

Access to Medicines

Oxfam International is a confederation of 12 organizations working together with over 3,000 partners in more than 100 countries to find lasting solutions to poverty, suffering and injustice. They point out that when patented medicines are priced out of the reach of poor patients—and out of the reach of their governments, many of which can't afford to spend more than a few dollars per person per year on healthcare—people suffer or die needlessly.

As one international worker asks, "It's a matter of values: Does the right of a corporation to earn a profit on its new product count more than the lives of millions of people? Shouldn't the balance between innovators' interests and the community's interest be protected somehow from such inaccessible pricing?"[36]

In many poor countries, few people have health insurance and spending on drugs comprises 50 to 90 percent of household costs for health care. In Burkina Faso, one of the poorest countries in West Africa, drugs account for over 80 percent of the spending on health each year. Annual government spending on health care in many low-income countries is usually $5 to $7 per person. In many wealthy countries, it is $1,600.[37]

Consumers in rich countries spend more than $2.2 billion per year on the drug Claritin, used to treat the symptoms of hay fever. That is more than the total annual expenditure on drugs in all of sub-Saharan Africa.[38]

Though providing access to needed medicines is a huge problem worldwide, there is actually at least one easy way you can help. Older medicines or outdated or old medical supplies and equipment in America are all frequently discarded because there is no viable means to get them to charities that need them. There is always a need for people who can act as "brokers" between the U.S. medical industry and a host of service organizations that get these medicines and supplies from America to places around the world where there is need. Here are two good groups to explore as a place to start. There are also many others:

- Project Cure (www.projectcure.org)
- Medical Assistance Program (www.map.org)

Access to Clean Water

Every day we drink water from our sink. Some of us prefer to filter it or buy bottled water. But for more than 1 billion people on our planet, access to clean water is only a dream. Study after study has shown that whenever a community improves its water supply, hygiene, sanitation and health improve dramatically. For example, the occurrence of diarrhea (a life killer in many parts of world) can be reduced by as much as 26 percent when basic water, hygiene and sanitation are supplied to a village. Despite this fact, the current statistics tell a terrible story. Forty percent of the world's 6 billion people have no acceptable means of sanitation, and more than 1 billion people draw their water from unsafe sources.[39]

The World Health Organization says diarrhea-related diseases remain a leading cause of illness and death in the developing world. Every year, about 2.2 million people die from diarrhea. Ninety percent of these deaths are among children, mostly in developing countries. A significant number of deaths are due to a single type of bacteria, shigella, which causes dysentery or bloody diarrhea. It is readily controlled by improving hygiene, water supply and sanitation. Although no vaccine exists and antibiotics may be inaccessible to many people, an effective intervention is available. The simple act of washing hands with soap and water reduces shigella and other types of diarrhea by up to 35 percent.[40]

Economic Injustice

According to the World Bank, half the world's people live on less than two dollars a day. Over one billion of these live on less than a dollar per day.[41] The assets of the 200 richest people in 1998 were more than the total annual income of 41 percent of the world's people.[42] Three families—Bill Gates, the Sultan of Brunei and the Walton family—have a combined wealth of some $135 billion. Their combined value equals the annual income of 600 million people living in the world's poorest countries.[43]

Get this: The richest one-fifth of the world:
- consumes 45 percent of all meat and fish, while the poorest fifth consumes 5 percent;
- consumes 58 percent of total energy, while the poorest fifth consumes less than 4 percent;
- has 74 percent of all telephone lines, while the poorest fifth has 1.5 percent;
- consumes 84 percent of all paper, while the poorest fifth consumes only 1.1 percent; and
- owns 87 percent of the world's vehicles, while the poorest fifth owns less than 1 percent.[44]

The "share" of the total global income among the poorest 20 percent of the world's people now stands at a miserable 1.1 percent, down from 1.4 percent in 1991 and 2.3 percent in 1960. It continues to shrink. On the other end of the spectrum, the ratio of the income of the top 20 percent to that of the poorest 20 percent rose from 30 to 1 in 1960, to a startling new high of 78 to 1 in 1994.[45]

Here is another way to put it that may make the situation clearer. If we could shrink the earth's population to a village of precisely 100 people, with all the existing human ratios remaining the same, it would look something like this:

- There would be 57 Asians, 21 Europeans, 14 from the Western Hemisphere (both north and south), and eight Africans.
- Fifty-two would be female; 48 would be male.
- Seventy would be non-white.
- Seventy would be non-Christian.
- Six individuals would posses 59 percent of the world's wealth... and all six of them would be from the United States.
- Eighty would live in substandard housing.
- Seventy would be unable to read.
- Fifty would suffer from malnutrition.
- Only one would have a college degree.
- Only one would own a computer.

I share these facts not to overwhelm you, but because we as followers of Jesus must be educated. This information just scratches the surface, but I hope it will impress upon you the severity of issues around the world that demand both our concern, attention, and response. I believe we act upon what we know and understand. I realize that sharing statistics like these can have the tendency to make us feel paralyzed and overwhelmed. This is where the Holy Spirit must inspire and empower our minds and hearts to receive this information and then pray for wisdom on how we can respond effectively.

Injustice among Ethnic Groups

So far I've focused on issues that impact billions on our planet. But there are also important issues of injustice and oppression that target specific ethnic groups across the globe. Many ethnic groups around the world— from all religions—face oppression and severe injustice on a daily basis. We as Christians should speak out against such ethnic oppression—even when the victims are not Christian. Here are brief descriptions of some of the ethnic groups facing oppression today. Many times these ethnic groups have few Christians among them. Great opportunities for empowerment and ministry exist when we speak out on their behalf, advocate for their cause, and serve them in the name of Jesus Christ.

> • **The Saharawi People.** In the northwest corner of the Sahara Desert live eight indigenous tribes collectively referred to as the Saharawi. They are a people who have suffered incredible injustice and hardship. Centuries ago they lived semi-nomadic lives in the Sahara and along the coastal areas of what is now Western Sahara, formerly the Spanish Sahara, the last African colony. When Spain decolonized Western Sahara in 1975 at the urging of the United Nations, Morocco invaded, engaging in genocide and occupying the Saharawi land and homes. Thousands of Saharawi fled on foot across the Sahara. They found refuge across the Algerian border where they set up four refugee camps with the help of the United Nations.

More than 165,000 Saharawi have lived in these refugee camps for nearly 30 years, completely dependent on outside aid for food, shelter and water. Despite the extremes of the Sahara where temperatures soar over 135 degrees in the summer and drop to below freezing in the winter, the Saharawi have survived. They have formed a nation-in-exile that is recognized by nearly 70 nations. In 1965 the United Nations General Assembly called for the independence of the Western Sahara, and in 1966 the International Court of Justice ruled that the Saharawi have the right to self determination. The Saharawi and Morocco agreed to a U.N.-negotiated ceasefire in 1991 to allow for a referendum to determine the will of the Saharawi people. This referendum has been repeatedly delayed by Morocco and has still not taken place.[46]

It is an amazing story and the Saharawi are a beautiful people. I visited there a few years ago and was touched deeply by their sincerity and genuineness. To further educate yourself on the struggles of the Saharawi, or to get involved, visit www.homelandonline.org. A good friend of mine can tell you all you want to know and show you how you can help.

• **The Tibetan People.** The Tibetan people have faced a great degree of injustice and oppression. In 1949, China began to put pressure on Tibet, declaring that it was not an independent nation, but an "estranged" part of "motherland China." From the late 1940s through the 1950s, Mao Tse Tung employed the Chinese military in a gradual "squeeze play," which has culminated in the loss of Tibet as a sovereign nation, the extermination of at least a million lives, and the displacement of hundreds of thousands.

The Tibetan culture has been all but wiped out inside China. In addition, China has put crippling restrictions on religious practice inside Tibet and has implemented an educational system that has virtually rewritten Tibetan history from the perspective of the Chinese Communist Party. As a result of the Chinese government's systematic destruction of Tibetan religious life, of the 6,000 monasteries that once thrived in Tibet, only 13 remain today.[47]

In 1959, the spiritual and political leader of Tibet, the 14th Dalai Lama, was forced to flee Lhasa (the capital of Tibet) during an uprising in which thousands of Tibetans were massacred. He traveled over the Himalayas, eventually arriving at the Indian border. The Indian government received him with open arms, eventually providing him with a home in exile among the hills above

Dharamsala and in the village of McLeod Ganj. This began a close relationship between India and the people of Tibet.

Hundreds of thousands of refugees having followed the Dalai Lama's footsteps across the snowcapped Himalayas during the last five decades. Today, there are still an average of 1,500 refugees making the journey each year toward India and Nepal. Tibetans have endured unspeakable horrors, and what most of the world does not realize is, their story of persecution is not just a part of history, it continues to this very day. The steady stream of refugees leaving Tibet for Nepal and India includes former political prisoners who have been beaten, raped and abused for years because of their cries for freedom and dignity in the face of an oppressive regime.

• **The Dalits of India.** In India there are approximately 250 million Dalits or "untouchables." This means that 25 percent of the population in India is Dalit. It also means that in a country where everybody is supposed to have equal rights and opportunities, one out of every four people is condemned as untouchable.

This tragedy is a direct consequence of India's caste system, which has remained entrenched in Indian culture for thousands of years. At the top are the Brahmins, the priests and arbiters of what is right and wrong in matters of religion and society. Next come the Kshatriyas, who are soldiers and administrators. The Vaisyas are the artisan and commercial class, and finally, the Sudras are the farmers and the peasant class.

These four castes are said to have come from Brahma's mouth (Brahmin), arms (Kshatriyas), thighs (Vaisyas) and feet (Sudras). Beneath the four main castes is a fifth group, the Scheduled Caste. They literally have no caste. They are the untouchables, the Dalits, which means oppressed, downtrodden and exploited as a social group. A Dalit is not considered to be part of human society, but is instead something beneath it. Dalits are seen as polluting for higher caste people. If a higher caste Hindu is touched by an untouchable or even had a Dalit's shadow cross them, they consider themselves to be polluted and have to go through a rigorous series of rituals to be cleansed.

The Dalits perform the most menial and degrading jobs. They are typically poor, deprived and socially backward. They do not have access to enough food, health care, housing or clothing. They do not have equal access to education or employment. And they face considerable injustices in every day life.

Officially, everybody in India has the same rights and opportunities, but in practice the reality, things are quite different. The Dalits are the poorest of the poor in the world and their caste status effectively strips them of their humanity. Dalits are denied access to public wells and public parks, and many restaurants use separate drinking glasses for Dalits. The ruling caste tells them they are Hindu, yet they are denied access to the temples, cannot become temple priests, and, due to lack of education, cannot even read the scriptures. Their women are sold into bonded prostitution. Even finding a place to bury their dead is a problem. Seventy percent of Dalits live below the poverty line.

On November 4, 2001 thousands of Dalits traveled to New Delhi from all over India to denounce the oppressive system in which they have been living. Even though the government tried to block the ceremony, a mass of people representing Dalits from all across India openly declared they were leaving Hinduism for religions that allowed them freedom and gave them equality. Since then, Dalits have regularly been identifying themselves with other faiths. Many states in India are passing or trying to pass local laws that prohibit the Dalits from converting to other religions.

Movements among the Dalits to leave the caste system have occurred in the past. Most did not have a lasting effect. Only in those areas where the Dalits became part of a new religious community did the change continue for generations.

The Dalits are crying out for wholistic reformation. Individuals and organizations from across India are rising to the great need of the Dalits. But it will take the effort of people from all over the world, partnering with those in India to see this movement have a sustaining effect on the fabric of the country. Since the majority of Dalits are illiterate, education is central to any program.

The vast majority of secondary schools in India are English. In order for the Dalits to gain acceptance to these schools and to be able to function in the marketplace, Dalits need English taught in primary schools. Beyond schooling, the Dalits need basic medical care, micro loans for business development, and people who will show them love and concern.

When responding to an ethnic group or a nation that has faced oppression and injustice, perhaps the place to start is to ask for forgiveness on behalf of former "westerners" who contributed to the problems or who showed a lack of concern, rather than acting as agents of positive change. This is especially helpful to remember if you find yourself talking to someone from a certain nation or ethnic group that has faced oppression and injustice. In fact, it is difficult to find an oppressed people group to whom this approach does not apply. For instance, in any Muslim region of the world, there is still deep animosity towards western influence and government policy. This concern is based on hundreds of years of history, in which many who claimed to be "Christian" did horrible things in the name of religion.

Beginning in the 11th Century and continuing through the 13th Century, Christians launched a series of armed expeditions, or Crusades, throughout the Arab world because the West wanted to free the Holy Land from Islamic influence. Most all of the Muslim world recalls this history; it is embedded deep into their psyche.

Even today, Muslim communities see oppression and injustice going on before their very eyes from those they perceive as western Christians. In the 1990s, the ethnic cleansing in Kosovo was an example. Do you ever wonder how the Muslim world views the ethnic cleansing in Kosovo? Ninety-five percent of all Albanians who were "ethnically cleansed" in Kosovo were Muslim. Who were their killers? Serbians who were orthodox Christian by ethnic and cultural identity.

Religion has been used as a tool for oppression for centuries. As one scholar put it, "Religion is not merely adherence to creeds or doctrines. Religion is the fundamental shaper of human life, social structures and systems; sometimes positively so, sometimes not." We, as Christ's followers, need to seek out opportunities to act as ambassadors of forgiveness toward the oppressed people of the world... so that doors may be re-opened for the Gospel to be shared.

When they think of a Christian, many Muslims in the world do not know the difference in practice and belief between Slobodan Milosevic and Billy Graham. Milosevic, a Serbian Christian, was tried for genocide against Muslims. When ministering with or around Muslims, you should always remember this fact—and sensitively, yet boldly, let them know that you do not agree with everything Christians have done to Muslims throughout history. You will be amazed at their open response, and the opportunity for trust and relationship that will come as a result.

I have found this to be true as I have talked to Muslims throughout the entire world. Many of us in the western Christian world may only want to think about and discuss what certain people within the Muslim world have done to us in the West, but let us not forget history and what we, the "Christian West," have done to Muslims throughout history.

Not only do the Crusades hinder our ability as Christians to impact certain people groups who are oppressed, but western colonization does as well. Before colonization ended in the mid 20th Century, many regions of the world were governed and controlled by western governments, mostly in Europe. The Dutch in Indonesia, Spain in the Philippines, the British throughout Africa and Asia, and the French in Africa. During these centuries of colonization, many of these European countries realized the importance of Christian missionaries to help set up education and commerce. We owe a great deal of debt and honor to the western missionaries who pioneered, suffered and served in the 19th Century.

However, most of them did not *just* bring the hope and love of the Gospel of Christ, but they also brought their culture, both the good and bad of it. Look at David Livingstone, the famous British missionary who served and explored Africa. During his missionary service, he believed he was not to stay in one place but to go on "God's Highway" as he called it. Livingstone wrote, "I must move on. I will bring Christianity, commerce and civilization to the people of Africa."[48] I would add that he also brought his culture with him, as anyone does who moves to another culture.

We never become 100 percent separate from our home culture when we move to another country. Many people in the world despise the West today as a result of those days of colonization and the impact it had on their local culture.

When I travel throughout India, especially the poorer and less educated parts of India, everyone assumes I am British, simply because India was colonized by Britain for 300 years. England did many good things during that time—such as establishing hospitals, creating the train system, improving education and so on. However, with those benefits also came missionaries who were perceived by the Indians as determined to change their culture or who were after the resources of the local people for their own gain. It's critical for us to understand these issues as we move out to minister and love individuals and entire ethnic groups who face injustice from those in power.

In addition to seeking understanding and asking forgiveness, we must also speak up on behalf of those who are oppressed, and do what we can to help them. When you speak out for different people groups who have faced injustice from other political regimes or governments, do not be afraid to speak your mind. Just be sure to speak with great caution and wisdom.

Remember Jesus' advice to His disciples in Matthew 10:6: "I am sending you out like sheep among wolves. Therefore, be as shrewd as snakes and innocent as doves."

Acts of injustice and oppression are usually rooted in political motivations—a desire to control money, land or power in government. For that reason we must use wisdom when speaking out in support of the oppressed—especially if you are living in an area like this and doing ministry. I have seen far too many western workers jeopardize their ministry and get thrown out of a country because they did not use wisdom when openly proclaiming their support for one political side or the other.

Try to do your work of ministry "through the conflict" as opposed to speaking out in support of a certain side of a conflict. In other words, whatever direction the political process goes, use caution when you speak your mind, especially if you are living in that country. By openly proclaiming your political opinion to those in your community, you will potentially isolate yourself from others who need Christ but who do not share your viewpoint. We should strive to do the work of the Kingdom no matter what is going on—in peace or war, famine or prosperity.

We Are the Means to Rescue People

God works through people. He could have chosen to work through angels, but He chose to work through you and me—flawed and needy as we are. Through the ages, God has taken broken people and made them whole. He has taken abused people and healed them of their pain and allowed them to minister grace and love to others. God wants to do the same with you.

Our God is a rescue God. He rescues us from our sin, death and despair and gives us hope, meaning and eternal life. God is in the business of taking people just like you and me and using them as conduits of hope and justice to the oppressed. We should not rely solely on the government to intervene. We should not look only to the "professional" minister or missionary to do the job. We are all participants with God in His mission in the world.

In Isaiah 58:6-10, God describes the kind of service He desires from all of us:

"Is not this the kind of fasting I have chosen: to loose the chains of injustice and untie the cords of the yoke, to set the oppressed free and break every yoke? Is it not to share your food with the hungry and to provide the poor wanderer with shelter—when you see the naked, to clothe him, and not to turn away from your own flesh and blood?

"Then your light will break forth like the dawn, and your healing will quickly appear; then your righteousness will go before you, and the glory of the Lord will be your rear guard. Then you will call, and the Lord will answer; you will cry for help, and he will say: 'Here am I.'

"If you do away with the yoke of oppression, with the pointing finger and malicious talk, and if you spend yourselves in behalf of the hungry and satisfy the needs of the oppressed, then your light will rise in the darkness, and your night will become like the noonday."

How Can I Rescue Them?

Praxis comes from the Latin term "to be put into practice." We should always look at the praxis of the Gospel in relationship to issues of justice or other issues in the Christian life. What does the Good News of Jesus Christ and His Kingdom mean for me, my family and my community? How can I put the Gospel into action?

In many cases, I believe that social justice activists or mission mobilizers have become too pragmatic in their requests for help—providing only a short list of their own ideas on what we should do and how we should do it, rather than simply explaining the full breadth of the need and allowing the Holy Spirit to direct people to act as they are inspired.

The Holy Spirit is always wanting to breathe creativity into the Church so that our original and fresh perspectives can be mobilized to provide a host of unique and potent agents for change, reconciliation and healing throughout the world. I have tried to both inspire you and explain to you why we should act justly and love mercy as followers of Jesus... as well as giving you some help in getting started. However, it is up to you to allow God to move on your heart and direct you on what he is specifically calling you to do. But whatever it is, **start now**!

- Start praying daily for God to give you wisdom, direction and vision.
- Gather a community to meet regularly to pray together and discuss issues of justice and ways to get others involved and educated.
- Go to your pastor and other church leaders and share what God is teaching you and ask if you can lead a "justice group" within your church. Hopefully, they will empower you and help you. If not, don't give up.
- Commit to pray daily for ministry workers who are working to respond to the issues of injustice in the world.
- Seek ways to raise money through an event, concert or sports tournament for a ministry that helps the oppressed.

Questions for Personal Reflection or Small Group Study:

1. Have you experienced a country in the world where people did not have access to clean water or good medicines? How did this make you feel? What did it make you want to do?

2. What verse in the Bible speaks to you the most when it comes to issues of justice? Why do you suppose that is?

3. Read and study the passage from Isaiah 58 quoted at the end of this chapter. What are the ways God is telling you to respond to injustice?

4. Can you remember the first time you really struggled with inequality in the world? What prompted the struggle? How might God have been speaking to you through that struggle?

5. Who do you know that you could ask to get together with you on a weekly basis to pray and talk about issues described in this chapter? How could taking this simple step help bring positive change to the world?

Notes

1. Gary Haugen, *Good News About Injustice: A Witness of Courage in a Hurting World* (Intervarsity Press, Colorado Springs, CO, 1999), 45
2. Ecclesiastes 4:1
3. John 17:3-4
4. Psalm 33:5
5. Jeremiah 9:24
6. Psalm 11:7
7. Isaiah 61:8
8. Isaiah 1:17
9. Micah 6:8
10. Matthew 6:10
11. Hebrews 6:19
12. David Bosch. *Transforming Mission* (Orbis, Maryknoll, NY, 1996), 508
13. www.state.gov
14. www.worldrevolution.org
15. www.state.gov
16. Under Secretary of State for Global Affairs Paula J. Dobriansky, in a speech given at the "Stop Child Trafficking: Modern-Day Slavery" Conference in Helsinki, June 2003
17. Penelope Saunders, "Sexual Trafficking and Forced Prostitution of Children," October 29, 1998
18. www.globalmarch.org
19. Penelope Saunders, "Sexual Trafficking and Forced Prostitution of Children," October 29, 1998
20. James 1:27
21. Jeremiah 21:12
22. from the United Nation's Office of High Commissioner of Human Rights, "Fact Sheet No. 14, Contemporary Forms of Slavery"

23. www.hrw.org
24. www.worldrevolution.org
25. Psalm 24:1
26. *Barnes' Notes*, Electronic Database (Biblesoft, Inc., 1997)
27. 1 Timothy 4:4-5
28. *Adam Clarke's Commentary*, Electronic Database (Biblesoft, Inc., 1996)
29. John 1:3
30. Colossians 1:16-17
31. Genesis 1:28, emphasis mine
32. www.worldrevolution.org
33. www.worldrevolution.org
34. www.oxfam.org
35. www.oxfam.org
36. www.oxfamamerica.org
37. www.oxfamamerica.org
38. www.accessmed-msf.org
39. www.worldrevolution.org
40. www.worldwatertoday.org
41. www.worldrevolution.org
42. UNDP Human Development Report, 1999
43. World Development Movement
44. United Nations Development Program: Human Development Report 1998
45. UNDP Human Development Report 1997
46. www.homelandonline.org
47. www.tibetanphotoproject.com
48. John Waters, *David Livingstone: Apostle To Africa* (Gospel Literature Service Publisher; Bombay, India; 1992), 13

A Different Kind of Power

"A Cherokee elder sitting with his grandchildren told them, 'In every life there is a terrible fight—a fight between two wolves. One is evil: he is fear, anger, envy, greed, arrogance, self-pity, resentment, and deceit. The other is good: joy, serenity, humility, peace, generosity, truth, gentleness, and compassion.' A child asked, 'Grandfather, which wolf will win?' The elder looked him in the eye. 'The one you feed.'"—Cherokee Proverb

"If we think of the Holy Spirit only as an impersonal power or influence, then our thought will constantly be, how can I get hold of and use the Holy Spirit; but if we think of Him in the biblical way as a divine Person, infinitely wise, infinitely holy, infinitely tender, then our thought will constantly be, "How can the Holy Spirit get hold of and use me? —R. A. Torrey

"Breath in me, O Holy Spirit, that my thoughts may all be holy. Act in me, O Holy Spirit, that my work, too, may be holy. Draw my heart, O Holy Spirit, that I love but what is holy. Strengthen me, O Holy Spirit, to defend all that is holy. Guard me, then, O Holy Spirit, that I always may be holy. "
—Augustine

"An Angelic Encounter" (*Blog Entry in early 2004*):

I recently took a short trip to India where I believe God was hearing the prayers of His people and sent an angel to save me from danger. It was a moment that left me truly humbled and thankful before God. I flew to New Delhi where I was to get on another flight to visit a ServLife worker serving among Tibetan refugees living in the mountains of northern India. My flight ended up being canceled so I took another plane. I flew to Kashmir, then hired a car to drive five more hours through three states to reach McLeod Ganj where the Dalai Lama lives along with 5,000 Tibetans in exile.

It was dark outside and after driving for several hours, my driver said he would take me no further. After realizing I could not convince him otherwise, he dropped me off about 40 miles short of my destination. I was forced to hop on the local public transportation, which in this case was a large 4-door jeep.

About eight men were in the vehicle. When I got in I began to pray. A very strong odor of alcohol was evident. Indeed, without knowing my situation, many of you were perhaps praying at this moment for me as well. After about 20 minutes of driving, we pulled off the main road and got on a dirt road for about another 20 minutes. After dropping off one man, a large crowd gathered around the vehicle and noticed me inside. A few of the men stood in front of the vehicle, effectively preventing it from moving forward. The situation did not make me nervous at first, but then a few of the men got into a heated argument over something as they were pointing to me and shouting at one another. The scene went from bad to worse very fast. I began to feel fear and thought I was about to become a victim of someone's hatred or greed—by either

*being hurt or killed by someone's weapon, or having all
of my belongings and money stolen.*

*All of the sudden as I looked up, there appeared
to be what looked like a woman in a white Indian dress (a
Sari). Her head was covered and there was a light
appearing on her, but I could not determine where the
light was coming from because our car lights were
pointing in another direction. She began to speak to the
crowd of angry men, who stopped their arguing to listen
to her. Then the men who were standing in front of the
vehicle inexplicably stepped to the side of the car.
Immediately, our driver hit the gas and drove off.*

*As we drove away, I looked back but could not
see the woman at all. I realized immediately that this was
an angel God had sent to protect me from danger. I cried
out in praise, thanking God for watching over me and
delivering me safely to my destination.*

*Be encouraged and know I thank all of you for
your prayers for us. PLEASE don't stop praying. Prayer
is the most important tool, resource and weapon we have—
far more than financial donations. Someone once asked
which is more important in our mission work—prayer or
funds—and I quickly responded, "If it's a choice between
one's prayer or penny, I always choose prayer. Always!"*

*Praise be to the Lord Jesus Christ who protects,
guides, sustains and watches those of us who claim Him
as Lord! He is our God, our Creator, Savior and King!
We worship our God in spirit and truth, and we don't bow
to idols made by the hands of people. We place our hope,
trust, life, confidence and faith in Him alone and believe
He will reveal and show His love, grace and compassion
to anyone who seeks Him with a sincere and pure heart.
Come Lord Jesus!*

The Bible says, "Make the Most High your dwelling—even the Lord, who is my refuge—then no harm will befall you, no disaster will come near your tent. For He will command His angels concerning you to guard you in all your ways; they will lift you up in their hands, so that you will not strike your foot against a stone."[1]

God is still doing miraculous things to cause His name to be known throughout the earth. Visions, healings, angelic encounters, demonic encounters and supernatural events were not just for the book of Acts in the Bible. In many places in the world, it isn't hard to find someone who came to Jesus Christ by having a dream or a vision or a miraculous healing. Many people ask me, "Why don't we see this in America more?"

My answer is always, "I have no idea." I do have some ideas, but I do not know the mind of God nor understand everything about how he works. No one does.

Eastern culture is typically not based on western, intellectual foundations. Belief in the supernatural and spirits are pervasive in most non-western cultures in the world—including the belief in witch craft, evil spirits and animism (the belief that spirits reside in objects). Although these beliefs are becoming more common in the West, they are still typically dismissed as irrational by most people. Perhaps God uses dreams, visions and healings more often in other places around the world because He knows these approaches are especially crucial for such supernaturally-minded people to come to faith in Jesus. He may also do it because the people of these cultures are more open to these realities than we are in the West.

The Spirit of God works in mysterious ways. Yet there are many issues around Pneumatology (the study of the Holy Spirit) that are crucial for all followers of Jesus to understand if we are to live in victory, be empowered for ministry, and commune and grow with God.

Misunderstanding the Holy Spirit

The Holy Spirit is often misunderstood among many followers of Jesus. Here are a few wrong views of the Holy Spirit I have heard people express:

• **The Holy Spirit exists to only punish me.** Some may think that the Holy Spirit exists only to hunt down those who do wrong and "get them." Like a cosmic policeman, these people believe the Holy Spirit's sole function is to seek out those who are doing wrong and punish them. This is a wrong view of the Holy Spirit. Yes, the Holy Spirit convicts us of sin. In John 16:8-9 the Bible says, "When the Spirit comes, He will convict the world of guilt in regard to sin and righteousness and judgment." Yet the Holy Spirit is not exclusively "someone" who is out to get you.

• **The Holy Spirit exists to make me feel good.** One One of the most common mistakes Christians make about the Holy Spirit is in relation to our emotions. The Holy Spirit does not exist solely to make us feel good or fill us with "warm, fuzzy" feelings. He comes to us to convict us of sin, to bring salvation and to empower us for ministry. Emotion may at times be a byproduct of the Holy Spirit's working in our lives—but it is not a prerequisite. Of course, we should not shun emotion in the Christian journey, but embrace it as one way (among many) that He communicates with us. Life is filled with emotions and, frankly, it would be boring without them. But for Christians, emotions are not an end in themselves, but should rather be seen as a tool God uses to transform our hearts, deepen our intimacy with Him, and produce fruit in our ministry to the world. The Holy Spirit will work through your emotions, but your emotions do not have to be in any particular "state" for the Holy Spirit to do His work.

• **The Holy Spirit makes normal people abnormal**. I have met some people who think they are more "spiritual" than others—at least they come across that way. Many times these "super spiritual" people don't relate well with others. They convey a sense of superiority and arrogance toward the rest of us. Rather than listen to your story humbly and compassionately, they claim to know God's plan for your life and don't hesitate to tell you what it is. This is not a genuine effect of being filled with the Holy Spirit; rather, it is just another expression of the flesh, cloaked in a spiritual façade. God does not want us to be so spiritually minded that we are of no earthly good. The Holy Spirit empowers us to love people—humbly and compassionately—in practical ways.

• **The Holy Spirit is unknowable and scary**. Some people fear the Holy Spirit. They picture Him as a mystical "ghost" who haunts them, working behind the scenes of their lives in mysterious and frightening ways. I have met some who actually fear what the Holy Spirit will do to them if they give their lives to God.

The Bible says, "For God did not give us a spirit of timidity [fear], but a spirit of power, of love and of self-discipline."[2] The Holy Spirit should not be feared, but pursued with your whole heart.

• **The Holy Spirit will only work in my life though a profound experience or encounter.** One of the mistakes believers make is to believe that every experience with the Holy Spirit must be dramatic and strike them like lightening from the clouds. While this is a possibility, the Spirit often works in far more subtle and quiet ways. That is one reason why silence is such a great spiritual discipline; very often we need silence to be aware of the Spirit of God and to hear Him. Psalm 46:10 says, "Be still, and know that I am God; I will be exalted among the nations, I will be exalted in the earth." Consider some of the ways God speaks in silence: A flower in bloom, a sunset over the ocean, the conception of a baby in a woman, a seed taking root... and the greatest tribute of all to the Holy Spirit's "quiet" work, the resurrection of Jesus Christ from the dead.

Understanding the Holy Spirit

I will not do justice in explaining all the workings of the Holy Spirit in this chapter. I will only scratch the surface. But I hope it will leave you hungry for more. I encourage you to read other books on the Holy Spirit and pray for the Holy Spirit to empower you, fill you, and reveal Himself to you, because He will. Perhaps there is no other issue as divisive as the nature of the Holy Spirit and His role in the Church today. Yet there is nothing else that can unite the Church besides the work of the Holy Spirit in a believer's life or in the Church.

Since the early days of the Church, the people of God have declared their belief and faith in the Holy Spirit. "I believe in the Holy Ghost, the Lord and Giver of life, which proceedeth from the Father and the Son, and with the Father and the Son together is worshiped and glorified." (from the Nicene Creed)

A.W. Tozer wrote, "The Spirit has will and intelligence and feeling and knowledge and sympathy and ability to love and see and think and hear and speak and desire as any person has."[3]

All through the Bible there are references to the Holy Spirit's nature, personhood and personality:

- "Where can I go from your Spirit? Where can I flee from your presence? If I go up to the heavens, you are there; if I make my bed in the depths, you are there."[4]
- "Jesus said, 'Therefore go and make disciples of all nations, baptizing them in the name of

the Father and of the Son and of the Holy Spirit.'"[5]

- "Flesh gives birth to flesh, but the Spirit gives birth to spirit."[6]
- "And I will ask the Father, and he will give you another Counselor to be with you forever—the Spirit of truth. The world cannot accept him, because it neither sees him nor knows him. But you know him, for he lives with you and will be in you."[7]
- "And if the Spirit of him who raised Jesus from the dead is living in you, he who raised Christ from the dead will also give life to your mortal bodies through his Spirit, who lives in you."[8]
- "…but God has revealed it to us by his Spirit."[9]

The chief function of the Holy Spirit is to illumine Jesus' teaching, to glorify His person, and to work in the life of the individual believer and the church.[10] The work of the Holy Spirit is always to exalt Jesus Christ. If you hear someone talking about the Holy Spirit in a way that does not put emphasis on Jesus Christ, have caution. The Holy Spirit never exalts himself, but always works to magnify Jesus.

Because the Holy Spirit is the power by which believers come to Christ and see with new eyes of faith, He is closer to us than we are to ourselves.

In the Old Testament, the Hebrew word used for the Spirit of God is *ruach*, meaning "breath," "wind" or "breeze."[11]

While living in Nepal, I heard a story of an untrained pastor who told his church that everyone in his village had the Holy Spirit. He had heard that the word spirit meant breath and went on to explain to his people that if they held their hand in front of their mouths they would feel the "Holy Spirit" coming out. Of course, this was incorrect teaching. The Holy Spirit is not the actual breath that comes out of your mouth.

The word for "Spirit" always used in the New Testament is *pneuma*, which means "wind or spirit."[8] In the New Testament, we find also the expressions, "the Spirit of God," "the Spirit of the Lord," "the Spirit of the Father," "the Spirit of Jesus," and the "Spirit of Christ."

The Holy Spirit is the third person in the Trinity. He is fully God. He is eternal, omniscient (all knowing), omnipresent (everywhere at all times), has a will and can speak. He is alive. He is a person. He is not particularly visible in the Bible because His ministry is to bear witness of Jesus Christ.

Understanding a Life of Mission Through the Sending of the Holy Spirit

The Christian life was not meant to be lived in isolation from the world. We are meant to practice missional habits and lifestyles that lead us to actively engage with people in all cultures. One of the dangers that has come from the rise of the Christian "subculture" in the West is the desire to withdraw from the lost and interact only with other Christians.

The word mission comes from the Latin word that means "to be sent." The word mission is not really in the Bible, but the theme is all throughout the Bible. God sent His Son to the earth (John 3:16). The Son sent the Spirit (John 20:22). The Triune God (Father, Son and Holy Spirit) sends all of us into the world to proclaim the goodness and grace of God found in Jesus Christ. The Holy Spirit's work in our lives is key to understanding mission because it is the Holy Spirit who empowers us to live a life of mission, leading us to go boldly into the myriad cultures of the world to demonstrate and proclaim the love of Christ. Here is an overview of some of the primary ways the Holy Spirit works in and through our lives:

• **The Holy Spirit reveals God to us and empowers us to become like Christ.** The Holy Spirit reveals to Christians the deep things of God. The Bible says, "...but God has revealed it to us by His Spirit. The Spirit searches all things, even the deep things of God. For who among men knows the thoughts of a man except the man's spirit within him? In the same way no one knows the thoughts of God except the Spirit of God. We have not received the spirit of the world but the Spirit who is from God, that we may understand what God has freely given us."[13]

In the same way, the Holy Spirit also reveals to us the mystery of Christ. As the Apostle Paul explained, "...that is, the mystery made known to me by revelation, as I have already written briefly. In reading this, then, you will be able to understand my insight into the mystery of Christ, which was not made known to men in other generations as it has now been revealed by the Spirit to God's holy apostles and prophets."[14]

If we think we can become effective disciples of Jesus through our own will power, we will surely be disappointed. The Holy Spirit works in our hearts to accomplish what we cannot do through our own ability, education or determination. Though we must cooperate in the process, we are not the source of the transforming power. Rather, it is his power, at work in our souls, that changes us into the image of Christ

The soul is the inner life of a person, the seat of emotion, and the center of human personality. When we describe the soul, we often use words like "passion," "desire," "true self," "life," "living being," "emotion" and "longing." Among other things, the Bible often describes the soul as the seat of desire or "the will." For example: the desire for food (Deuteronomy 12:20-21), the desire for love (Song of Songs 1:7), the desire to long for God (Psalm 63:1), the desire to rejoice (Psalm 86:4), and the desire to know (Psalm 139:14).

Whenever people are transformed into the likeness of Jesus, their desires change. Their emotions change. Their passions change. Through the process of transformation, they leave behind their old life of selfishness, greed and lust, and take on more and more of Christ. This is the working of the Holy Spirit and not our own doing.

Are churches really producing people who are being transformed into the image of Jesus? Here is a little exercise to try, based on the Fruit of the Spirit listed in Galatians 5:22-24: "But the fruit of the Spirit is love, joy, peace, patience, kindness, goodness, faithfulness, gentleness and self-control. Against such things there is no law."

Think of the typical regular churchgoers in your community and ask yourself, "Are these people filled with love? Are they filled with joy?" and so on down through the entire list. What do you notice as you examine the evidence? What about for your own life? Are these the words that your best friend, spouse or family member would use to describe you?

We don't have to look very deep to realize that we all have a great deal of transformation to do. But to get there, we must adopt the same heart and attitude toward discipleship as the Apostle Paul demonstrated when he wrote: "...I am again in the pains of childbirth until Christ is formed in you."[15] We have to surrender and submit to the Holy Spirit who will work in us to remake us in the image of Christ.

• **The Holy Spirit helps us in our weakness.** "In the same way, the Spirit helps us in our weakness. We do not know what we ought to pray for, but the Spirit himself intercedes for us with groans that words cannot express."[16]

The Holy Spirit does in and through us what we cannot do by our own will or determination (Colosians 1:29). This is the mystery of the Holy Spirit. Yielding and trusting the work of the Holy Spirit is so key in the Christian journey. The Spirit enables us to pray and He works through us. He discloses to us our needs and wants, as well as our sins and shortcomings, so as to impress upon us a deep sense of our absolute dependence on God.

We are often not aware of our wants, and we have no deep desire for those supplies of grace which we really need. We are led to say with the Laodiceans, "I am rich and increased with goods, and have need of nothing;" not knowing that "...we are wretched, and miserable, and poor, and blind, and naked."[17] During our times of weakness, it is absolutely crucial to pray that the Holy Spirit will fill us and empower us with His supernatural presence. The theme is throughout Scripture, we have not because we do not ask in faith (James 1:6-7; James 4:2; 1 John 3:22; and 1 John 5:14).

• **The Holy Spirit empowers us to overcome the demonic and evil.** While ministering in India one year I was living at a local Bible college in Calcuta for several weeks. I enjoyed eating, worshiping, praying and getting to know all the students who came there from different parts of India. We had fun and would sneek up on the roof to trap pigeons for a late night snack (grilled pigeon is actually not that bad).

One day I was asked to go along with the students as they went out to do evangelistic outreach in the streets of Calcutta. Without hesitation, I said yes. It was a beautiful sight to see Indians preaching the Gospel to other Indians and passing out food and clothes. At one point they asked me to preach to the crowd that had gathered. I began to tell the crowd that I was no different than them, although I came from a different country. I told them that I needed God and needed forgivness of sin. After two or three minutes of preaching through an interpreter I began to notice that an Indian man who was standing next to my interpreter would talk loudly whenever the interpreter would speak.

The faces in the crowd looked confused and they did not know who to listen to, my interpreter or the other man. At first, I thought this man must be drunk but after a little observation, I could tell he was not. I began to sense a very evil spirit from this man and realized he was keeping the crowd from hearing the Gospel of Jesus.

Without hesitation, I looked directly at him and said, "In the name of Jesus Christ I command you to stop preventing these people from hearing about Jesus and leave this place." Immediately, the man walked away. The crowd saw this and was amazed. Honestly, so was I. The crowd grew as more and more people began to rush toward me to hear about Jesus. It was an amazing reminder of the reality of evil forces in the world and their efforts to keep people from hearing about Jesus Christ.

Christians tend to take one of two extremes when it comes to the demonic and evil. They either emphasize the devil too much, or else they don't focus enough on the reality of evil. The Christian's true place of strength rests in the middle ground between these two extremes. Paul admonished the believers in Ephesus to "...put on the full armor of God so that you can take your stand against the devil's schemes. For our struggle is not against flesh and blood, but against the rulers, against the authorities, against the powers of this dark world and against the spiritual forces of evil in the heavenly realms."[18]

During His ministry, Jesus referred to the Spirit of God (Matt 12:28-29; Luke 11:20) as the power by which He cast out demons, thereby invading the stronghold of Satan and freeing those held captive. In the same way, the Spirit works with the Father and Son in releasing the redeeming power of the Kingdom of God through us.[19]

So many people try to minister solely through their own strength—that is, their own ability, personality and talents. Certainly, God has blessed each of us with unique natural gifts and personalities. We are not all clones with identical abilities. God gifted Billy Graham differently than He did Mother Teresa. Whatever our natural gifts, however, we must surrender them to God and allow the Holy Spirit to equip us with His supernatural life and ministry. Only then will we have lasting fruit and be able to face evil in whatever form evil takes.

While many in the Christian family will continue to argue about exactly how evil manifests itself in the world, no follower of Jesus can deny that the enemy is alive and active. Whether evil manifests through an individual—like Adolph Hitler, Pol Pot of Cambodia or Saddam Hussein of Iraq—or in a more systemic way—through governments, organizations or companies—we must seek the wisdom of the Holy Spirit to guide our actions, words and steps so that the Gospel of Jesus Christ is free to bring sight to the spiritually blind and freedom to those in spiritual prison.

Another time while ministering in India, I was on the streets sharing Christ with my Indian friends. After a long day of preaching the Gospel, distributing food and praying for the sick, I experienced an amazing encounter I will never forget.

After we had been in a park playing a guitar and sharing about Jesus Christ for an hour or so, I looked down and saw a man who had legs as round as a pipe sitting at my feet. He could not walk and looked as if he lived on the streets. He was pulling at my pants trying to get my attention. At first, I did not know what he wanted or what he was trying to tell me. But then he began to point at his deformed legs and then up to the Bible I was holding in my hand, and then up at the sky. He did this about five times before I realized what he was trying to say: "If your God is powerful, have him fix my legs." I was overwhelmed with compassion. I was convinced that God was going to heal this man before the crowd of 50 or so Hindus who had been listening to us preach about Christ.

Our small team gathered around the man and began to pray fervently for him to be healed in the name of Jesus Christ so all the people gathered could see the power of the Gospel demonstrated. After praying, nothing happened. I left feeling so discouraged and defeated. "Why God?" I asked. "We have been preaching all day and sharing about Christ all over the city of Calcutta, and we prayed in faith that you would heal that man. Why?"

After wrestling with God over this, I heard God's still small voice in my soul, "I want you to be faithful in preaching the Gospel and praying for the sick. You are not called to be successful, just faithful. Be faithful."

It is a lesson I still remember to this day.

As followers of Christ, we are called to be faithful and obedient to whatever God leads us to do. That's all. The results are up to God. Paul wrote, "But the Lord is faithful, and he will strengthen and protect you from the evil one. We have confidence in the Lord that you are doing and will continue to do the things we command.

May the Lord direct your hearts into God's love and Christ's perseverance."[20]

• **The Holy Spirit empowers us to speak the Gospel with boldness and clarity.** "And they were all filled with the Holy Spirit, and they spoke the word of God with boldness."[21] More than ever, I believe we need the filling of the Holy Spirit to articulate the Good News of Jesus with grace and love. We have the answer that saves people from addictions, eating disorders, and other behaviors that bring destruction. Jesus Christ alone can bring salvation, meaning, identity, security, and eternal life to people's hearts. We offer hope to the lonely, broken and rejected. Jesus Christ is this hope.

Earlier in the book, I wrote about the good and bad ways to talk to others about Jesus. May we be filled to live a life that speaks hope to others. May the Holy Spirit empower us to have conversations with our friends and family that inspire them to seek to know Jesus for themselves. As Paul said, "We proclaim him, admonishing and teaching everyone with all wisdom, so that we may present everyone perfect in Christ. To this end I labor, struggling with all his energy, which so powerfully works in me."[22]

• **The Holy Spirit gives us dreams and visions for our lives.** Vision makes people come alive. The Holy Spirit releases life-giving visions and dreams in God's people. When you hear someone cast a vision in the Spirit it truly does something powerful and inspirational for those who hear. Indeed the proverb from the Bible is true, "Where there is no vision, the people perish."[23]

We all want vision—vision for our life, marriage, church, work and ministry. I love to be around others with vision. I think vision is simply seeing what can become reality and not being stuck in what exists now. It is seeing the potential in someone else, an organization, a country, a church or a company. People with little vision seem incapable of seeing anything beyond the here and now. But those with vision see what is possible. It's the difference between the "real" and the "ideal."

What is the current reality and what is the ideal reality we can move toward? Regardless of whether it is a pastor sharing a vision for a church, a presidential candidate sharing for a nation, or a teacher sharing vision to a classroom of children, we all need to see not only what is, but also what can be. We need to know not only who we are right now, but, through God's power, who we can become. God said, "I will pour out my Spirit on all people. Your sons and daughters will prophesy, your old men will dream dreams, your young men will see visions."[24]

We need more dreamers and visionaries. Those who can articulate with clarity God's vision for His people are much needed. One of stumbling blocks of the church is its stubborn desire for the mundane and predictable. We want worship music that always sounds the same, sermons that all sound alike, and people who talk like everyone else.

There is lack of vision in the missionary enterprise as well. There is a great need for Spirit-led authenticity and uniqueness in our dreams and visions for reaching a world for Jesus Christ. We need entrepreneurial missionaries who can pioneer innovative ministries and churches around the world. As Christian leaders, we do not need to have people simply follow our own ideas for their lives; rather, we need to help them identify their own unique path and calling, and then do all we can to help them get there.

When I first started ServLife many people did not understand what I was doing. Actually, some people still do not understand. For every one person who is excited and supportive of my work, there are three who do not get it and respond with confusion or disbelief. Many people over the years have expressed concern or confusion over why I did not simply join an existing ministry or missionary organization. One gentlemen once asked me, "Why did you start your own organization? Isn't that just reinventing the wheel?" I responded, "I sure hope so. We need some new wheels to get the job done, right?" He just looked at me, obviously puzzled.

I believe there are many reading this book who have a dream for a ministry, a business, a nation or people group. My encouragement to you is this: GO FOR IT! Do not let anyone or anything stop you from letting God see your dream become a reality. Yes, seek counsel and advice from others. As Proverbs 15:22 says, "Plans fail for lack of counsel, but with many advisers they succeed."

Yes, people will discourage you—probably the ones you least expect. Many will offer little encouragement or give you the emotional support you need. Money may be short, but if God calls you, who can stop you?

Perhaps you are having trouble identifying what your calling is. The author Frederick Buechner gave a wonderful bit of wisdom about finding your calling when he wrote, "Your calling is where your greatest joys and the worlds greatest needs intersect."

When do you most feel alive? When is it that you experience the deepest sense of joy in what you are doing? Perhaps it is with children? Perhaps when you are in the mountains? Perhaps it is in another culture? Whatever it is, ask God to pour His Spirit upon it, and reveal to you how your passion can be used for His glory. And if you are having a hard time naming your greatest joy, pray to the Holy Spirit for revelation and He will hear your prayer.

God wants to give you purpose even more than you desire to receive it.

Here are some suggestions on how you can begin to dream:

•   Research cities and countries throughout the world that are less than 5 percent Christian. Dream about what it would take for that city or nation to become 20 percent Christian? What would be needed? What could you do to help inspire a change like that? How could you give your life to such a great cause?

•   It's estimated that every day about 30,000 people die from preventable diseases such as pneumonia, tuberculosis, measles and diarrhea. How could you spend your life getting this number reduced or even eliminated?

•   In Nepal, 9,000 to 10,000 Nepalese children, mostly between the ages of 10 and 18, are drawn into the sex traffic industry in India *every year*.[25] How could you change this? What could you do with your life to stop this great tragedy once and for all?

•   Cambodia suffers from an infant mortality rate of 135 deaths per 1,000 births. Compare this to the infant mortality rate of America, which is 1.2 deaths per 1,000 births. How might you reduce the infant mortality rate in Cambodia?

In the year 1806 a small group of young students at Williams College gathered to pray. As they prayed, a rainstorm hit, forcing the five students to run to a nearby haystack to keep dry. Once there, they continued to pray, and the Holy Spirit began to speak a vision to their hearts.

They committed themselves as a group "...to send the Gospel to the pagans of Asia, and to the disciples of Mohammed." By 1810, they had inspired the Congregationalists of Massachusetts and Connecticut to organize the American Board of Commissioners of Foreign Missions, America's first foreign missionary society. The famous missionaries Adoniram Judson and Luther Rice were a part of that first group of missionaries who were sent from America in 1812. All of this came from a vision received by a group of simple students, huddled by a haystack in the pouring rain.[26]

• **The Holy Spirit inspires our creativity.** The work of the Holy Spirit in our lives allows us all to be artists. Through the Spirit, I believe we all have the capacity to create beauty and inspire others—in a thousand different ways. Most people will say, "I am not an artist." But I would argue that we are all artists in Christ, for His Spirit empowers us all to create beauty through all we do.

Now we may not be able to earn a salary with what we create as some can, but we can use our creativity to offer hope and encouragement to others, or even inspire them to action. It may be through a simple greeting card you make yourself, a photograph you take, or a poem you write. Or perhaps your creativity lies in cooking, singing, relating to children, repairing cars, writing computer code, throwing parties, or one of a thousand other possible expressions. But whatever your creative bend, God can take what you have and make it something beautiful and inspiring for others in the world.

There is a great need for a revolution of creativity in the body of Christ. I pray that the Holy Spirit would be poured out on the Church in such a way that ordinary followers of Jesus would begin to see themselves as creative beings made in his image, and then be inspired to use their creativity to advance the cause of Jesus Christ on the earth. I believe people who do not know God are drawn to "holy creativity." When they see people who create out of love rather than merely for profit or recognition, I believe they will be inspired to seek out the source of that love—which is Jesus himself.

We as a mission organization are trying to empower and unleash artists within the body of Christ to help bring awareness and education to the body of Christ about global issues. One young man in the Midwest was determined to inspire children through photography. He wrote our office and asked for a small amount of start up capital so he could buy a few dozen disposable cameras. He spent a whole day teaching a group of several dozen children how to take photographs. They walked through the parks and streets taking photographs of interesting things they saw. They took photographs of other children as well.

About one week later he organized a public photo gallery of each child's two best photos. The proceeds from the sale of the photographs (mostly bought by the parents) were sent to our mission to support the work we do among orphanages. While teaching the children to be creative in photography, he was also educating them on children around the world and the many things they did not get to enjoy.

• **The Holy Spirit guides us in prayer.** Often times, when we do not see the fruit in ministry, it is because we are not praying right. I heard Peter Wagner tell a great story at Fuller Seminary on the need for strategic prayer.

Iraq invaded Kuwait in 1991 and later fired scud missiles into Israel. It is commonly known that the only way Saddam Hussein could find out where his scud missiles landed was by watching CNN. On the other hand,

American bombs were known as "smart bombs." They were guided to their specific targets by a sophisticated laser targeting system. I've heard it said that you can make a smart bomb fly hundreds of miles and land right on top of a dime, provided the laser is pointed at that dime. This is a great illustration of how many Christians pray. Some Christians' prayers are like Saddam's scud missiles. We just fire off ambiguous requests to God, hoping they will make a difference, but never really knowing whether they have any effect. On the other hand, some Christians know the power of guided, strategic prayers that make the demons of hell shake in their boots.

The Bible says, "For though we live in the world, we do not wage war as the world does. The weapons we fight with are not the weapons of the world. On the contrary, they have divine power to demolish strongholds. We demolish arguments and every pretension that sets itself up against the knowledge of God, and we take captive every thought to make it obedient to Christ."[27]

We must learn to wage war, not in an aimless way, but with specific and guided prayers, allowing the Holy Spirit to guide us. We cannot rely on our own ideas, money, our own political agenda or on common sense. We must allow the Holy Spirit to use us as people of prayer.

Here are a few guidelines to help you pray strategically in the Holy Spirit:

Pray with other people. We should not wage war alone. Satan and all his demons are scared to death when followers of Jesus gather to pray. They could care less if we just got together to eat, talk and laugh. But when we pray together and agree with each other in prayer, watch out. Jesus said "Again, I tell you that if two of you on earth agree about anything you ask for, it will be done for you by my Father in heaven. For where two or three come together in my name, there am I with them."[28]

When you gather with others to pray it is helpful to remind your group about the power of agreement. Whenever someone is praying, encourage others in the group to say aloud things like "I agree," "Yes," or "Amen," which simply means "so be it." You don't have to shout or to be disruptive, but speak loudly enough so that the one who is praying knows you are agreeing with his or her prayer to God.

When confronted with evil, talk to Jesus first. When you come across evil in your own life or in someone else's life, you should pray to Jesus first and not try and address the demonic directly. Allow Jesus Christ to be the center of your thoughts and begin to worship and focus on His greatness. Ask Him to guide you and lead you in what you should do. Perhaps sing a song you know that brings Jesus to the center. The darkness does not like the light. And when the light of Christ is brought before our minds and hearts, there is power there. Jesus Christ defeated Satan at the cross and at the resurrection. This is where the memorization of Scripture is vital. When you sense the presence of evil in your own heart or in the heart of someone around you, begin to speak Scripture that you have memorized. A few passages to start with are:

"You, dear children, are from God and have overcome them, because the one who is in you is greater than the one who is in the world."[29]

"They overcame him by the blood of the Lamb and by the word of their testimony; they did not love their lives so much as to shrink from death."[30]

"The weapons we fight with are not the weapons of the world. On the contrary, they have divine power to demolish strongholds. We demolish arguments and every pretension that sets itself up against the knowledge of God, and we take captive every thought to make it obedient to Christ."[31]

And as you confront evil, always remember: Jesus has the ultimate power over evil and is our greatest weapon against evil.

When you pray for someone who does know God, ask God to give them eyes to see. The Bible says, "The god of this age [Satan] has blinded the minds of unbelievers, so that they cannot see the light of the gospel of the glory of Christ, who is the image of God."[32] When we have friends and family members who do not know or love God, we must learn to pray that the blindfolds Satan has placed over their eyes will be removed. We must pray specific prayers in order to see specific change. This same principle applies as we pray for whole cities and nations.

A Dream for a New and Different Stereotype of Missionaries

If you've been around the church for very long, then I'm sure you've heard the stereotypical description of a missionary. You know, the old man (or sometimes woman) who is awkward and socially inept, dresses funny, and takes a strange delight in showing slides for hours on end. Who would want to be like that?

I often wonder what it will take to bury this stereotype once and for all. I believe it can be done, and more importantly, that it *should* be done. We should not have to be wasting our energy trying to deconstruct this old, false stereotype, which still manages to turn many people away from pursuing or supporting global missions. The actual reality of what mission work is today, and what missionaries are really like, is dramatically different from the image this old stereotype projects.

I can't wait for the day when the stereotype finally dies away, and everyone who thinks of a missionary will picture people who are both young and old, articulate, filled with life, fun to be around, and on a quest for adventure like no other.

I pray that if you are reading this book and struggling with a hunger and passion to be involved in the mission of God around the world, no matter how old or young you are, that you will not wait any longer. Go for it now! I plead with you to step out, jump in and get your hands dirty, and learn as you go. Don't stop and stay still too long and try to figure it all out. My hunch is that if you have the desire, then God is already at work in your heart, and will show you the way.

If you don't have the desire, then maybe you will after reading this book. God is speaking to ordinary people and allowing them to do extraordinary things in His name and for His glory around the earth today. You could be one of them.

Perhaps you already are.

Questions for Personal Reflection or Small Group Study:

1. How might the Holy Spirit use your creativity to bless others?

2. Have you ever heard teaching on the Holy Spirit that was not accurate? What was it? How did you determine it wasn't the truth?

3. Have you ever heard someone share a dream inspired by the Holy Spirit? If so, what was it?

4. What dreams do you believe the Holy Spirit is leading you to pursue? If you can't think of one, what sort of dream would you really love the Holy Spirit to give you for your life?

5. What's one thing you deeply desire for your life— something that you know will take the power of the Holy Spirit to accomplish? What do you think God is saying to you about that desire?

Notes
1. Psalm 91:9-12
2. 2 Timothy 1:7
3. A.W. Tozer, *Being filled with the Holy Spirit* (Christian Publications, 1972), 24
4. Psalms 139:7-8
5. Matthew 28:19
6. John 3:6
7. John 14:16-18
8. Romans 8:11
9. 1 Corinthians 2:10
10. *Nelson's Illustrated Bible Dictionary* (Thomas Nelson Publishers, 1986)
11. *International Standard Bible Encyclopedia*, Electronic Database (Biblesoft, Inc., 1996)
12. *New American Standard Updated Edition Exhaustive Concordance of the Bible with Hebrew-Aramaic and Greek Dictionaries* (The Lockman Foundation, 1998)
13. 1 Corinthians 2:10-12
14. Ephesians 3:3-5
15. Galatians 4:19
16. Romans 8:26
17. Revelation 3:17
18. Ephesians 6:11-13
19. *Nelson's Illustrated Bible Dictionary* (Thomas Nelson Publishers, 1986)
20. 2 Thessalonians 3:3-5
21. Acts 4:31
22. Colossians 1:28-29
23. Proverbs 29:18 (KJV)
24. Joel 2:28
25. U.S. State Department, Human Rights Report, 1999
26. Ken Curtis PH.D., Beth Jacobson, Diana Severance Ph.D., Ann T. Snyder and Dan Graves, *GLIMPSES* (*Christian History Institute,* 2003)
27. 2 Corinthians 10:3-6
28. Matthew 18:19-20
29. 1 John 4:4
30. Revelation 12:11
31. 2 Corinthians 10:4-5
32. 2 Corinthians 4:4

Appendix
A

Stories from Around the World

I thought you would enjoy reading some other stories and encounters from around the world and allow them to speak for themselves. They demonstrate God's faithfulness and grace. Some of them will just bring you a smile to your face.

My Grandfather Known in New Delhi, India

I was in India for several months and received a fax from my father. (This is before email.) I learned that a friend of my father's from Houston, Chris Bryan, was doing business in India. I met with Chris and he introduced me to some of his Enron colleagues from America who were working in India. After several months of living on a meager budget and sleeping in $2/night hostels, I was the guest of a couple from Texas for a few days. I sat down the first night in their apartment in New Delhi and could not believe the smells coming from the kitchen. A roast, green beans, mashed potatoes and tastes from back home. After enjoying a wonderful dinner and conversation, this man who I had just met began to think and remembered that the name Vestal sounded familiar to him, but could not recall from where. He then began thinking aloud, not realizing for sure if his memory was correct, "I think I remember as a young boy that an evangelist came to our church and he had a scar on his face and he led me to Christ... I think his name might have been Vestal."

"Yes! That was my grandfather," I exclaimed. "He burned his face real bad as a baby and had over 20 plastic surgeries before he turned 18. It left a big scar on his face."

We realized we were spiritually related and had an amazing connection. I stayed just for a few short days to rest and ate a lot of apple pie before venturing back to visit my friends in the villages. As nice as it was, I missed the long train rides, sleeping on hard beds and eating rice and *daal.*

A Boy Named Daniel in the Philippines

Right after I graduated from college, I took off for about six months to go to Asia. I spent about six weeks of this time in the Philippines. I was able to minister and live with several wonderful Philipino families. My time in Manila was with a pastor and his family. After one Sunday of preaching and ministering in the church, a woman came up to me holding her son. She asked me if I was related to Daniel Vestal who had come to the Philippines about 30 years earlier. I told her that this was correct. She began to tell me that she remembered how he (my father) stayed with her family, and she heard him preach when she was a young girl. My father went to the Philippines when he was in college back in the 1960s. She began, "Your father led me to Christ one day after I heard him preach. He made such an impact on me that I named my first son after him. I wanted to meet you and introduce you to my Daniel."

I was moved to tears and we shared the day together. What a wonderful, divine moment of encouraging each other.

Engagement in Cairo

When I met my wife for the first time, I knew before she did that we would be married one day. Her beauty, her love for God and the poor, and her mobility were all qualities that really attracted me to her. We had the opportunity to travel together in the Middle East on a mission while we were dating. The one thing she did not know was that I had an engagement ring with me, though we had only been dating for several short months.

As I was struggling and praying to God whether this was the right moment, I found myself alone in Aqaba, Jordan. Elise traveled back to Amman, Jordan with some of our Arabic friends, and I was left to really make the decision. As I wandered into a Chinese restaurant in an Arabic country, I was welcomed by a Hispanic singer on cassette, Julio Iglesias. As I sat, eating alone, "our song" came on, "Only fools Rush In," by Elvis Presley. I could not believe it. My decision was made and Julio helped me make it.

I proposed in Cairo before she flew back to America. We flew back to Cairo around noon and had the whole day together before Elise left around midnight. I had the whole day planned—an engagement story that would top anyone's. We spent the day riding horses around the pyramids and then ate dinner on a boat going down the Nile River, by candlelight.

As the time approached, I took Elise to the edge of the boat and played her our song. Yes, it was Julio. I had written a poem and got down on my knees and proposed. Well, I wish I could end the story for all you romantic readers with a "she said yes" and we hugged, but that is not what happened. Instead, she said she needed more time, and I was crushed and rejected like never before.

We got back in the car and went to the airport. It wasn't the best time to depart, with all that had happened. Elise cried the whole way to the airport, fearing she might not ever see me again. We were not able to talk on the way. Once we got there, I realized I had about one hour to assure her of my love.

Well it did not work out like that. She got stuck behind security and they would not let her through. The Egyptian customs chief told me he was about to take me to jail because I was yelling and getting angry for them not allowing her through. When we asked if she could come out to give me a hug, the answer was no. Elise began to cry and finally they let her go, but we were not able to talk through things at all. I remember shouting to her through the Egyptian armed guards and security, "Don't worry. I love you. We don't have to have it all figured out, and we can work through this."

My last site of her was her beautiful smile leaving for Amsterdam. Oh mind you, she did take the ring after the Egyptian customs official I asked to carry it to her, did. After that, we ended up getting "officially" engaged a few months later under an oak tree in Houston, Texas and were married just a few months after that.

It was worth the fight and the wait, but indeed, our Cairo airport scene was certainly worthy of a scene in a movie. So gentlemen, if you have met the woman of your dreams and she does not know it yet, it's worth the patience and the pursuit of her heart.

On National Television in Baghdad

In 1996, I made it to Baghdad. Once we were there, we were taken to meet the Minister of Health. He was one of Saddam Hussein's cabinet members. We had brought with us more than $250,000 worth of medicine and left it with a Syrian orthodox church to distribute. Once arriving at the government office, I thought of all the times that this man had met with Saddam. To what degree had this man been a pawn in the hands of an evil dictator, denying the people of Iraq medical attention for the sake of political loyalty

As we sat down and began talking to the minister, I noticed an older video camera being used by one of the Iraqi staff. There was a bright light on it that seemed to not be working correctly. Not thinking much of the meeting or the old large video camera, we left our meeting to visit some hospitals in Baghdad. Later that evening, I went to a church in Baghdad to speak to a women's gathering when a church elder came to me and said, "Hey, I saw you on Iraqi television today meeting with the health minister."

Our short meeting landed on the nation's only television station that evening. I imagine what was said was propaganda to try and convince the people of Iraq to have deeper loyalty to the regime of Saddam, but who knows? All I know is that all of Baghdad has seen me on television.

A Knife to my Throat in Atlanta

Have you ever had a knife pulled on you while you were ministering to someone? I did—at age 17. At the time, I was volunteering weekly in Atlanta, Georgia where I would go downtown to share Christ and pass out items to the homeless. One night I will never forget a man pulled a knife on me and said, "Did you know a black man's blood is different than a white man's blood?" I was scared to death. I did not know what to do and thought I was about to die. I just began to pray and out came these words from my mouth, "I don't know about that, but I do know the blood of Jesus is for both the black man and the white man. The blood of Jesus makes the white man and black man friends and allows them to love each other."

All of a sudden he dropped his knife, hugged me and began to cry. Mind you, this was a 50-year-old black man hugging a young white suburban kid. It was an amazing night. I took him inside and bought him dinner, and he prayed to receive Christ.

Snuggling a Mango Tree into the U.S.

You have probably heard of missionaries smuggling Bibles into communist countries, but I'm sure you have never heard of missionaries smuggling mango trees into America. You see, America has strict laws against bringing fruits and plants across the border for fear of carrying a disease into the country. As I have written before, my college summer years were all spent in India, preaching and ministering with local Indian missionaries. One year I fell in love with mangoes. I literally ate them three to four times each day. I thought it would be a grand idea to try and take a mango tree back to my parents' house in Houston, Texas because I thought the weather conditions in Houston were similar to India's climate. In so doing, I figured I could come home to my parents for years to come and have fresh mangoes from my very own mango tree.

I even envisioned that I could bring my children home one day and we could all have mangoes together, and I could tell stories of my travels through India as a young guy.

When I told my Indian friend, Pushatom to help me carry several Mango trees back to America, he stared at me with a bit of confusion in his eyes, but he agreed to help. So for six hours, I drove around on his motorcycle looking for the exact size of mango trees that I could somehow get to Texas. After finding them, I wrapped them in newspaper to hide them. Getting them out of India was no problem, but flying into America I began to get a bit nervous about the customs form that asked if you are carrying fruits, plants or vegetables into the country. The decision before me was to be honest or dishonest. I checked the box, "YES, I do have these items.

As we arrived and stood in line to cross the customs official, I prayed, "God, please let me get these mango trees into the country. I have been suffering for you for months, sleeping on floors and sick beyond ways I knew were even possible." Well, I guess my prayer worked because the customs man waved us through without even looking at my customs card. I planted the trees in my parents' backyard, but they died during the winter. Believe it or not, it does get below freezing a few days during winter in Houston.

My First Visit to Raxaul

ServLife has a mission center in Raxaul, a town in northern India. It's a modest-sized town of about 150,000 to 200,000 people, not a large city for India. On my first visit to Raxaul, I had the most unique encounter. At that point in time, I had no idea I would be making many more trips there in the years to come. I got off a long, 30-hour train ride without much sleep. Not realizing I was in Raxaul, I complied when told to go to the police station. "For what?" I wondered. This was not an international border crossing. But I went.

Four hours later, I finally made it out. You would not believe how they searched our belongings. I remember one policeman squeezing toothpaste out of my toothpaste tube to see if it was legitimate toothpaste. On one occasion, I remember a policeman loading bullets into his gun right in front of where we were sitting. Many questions were asked.

Stepping out of the police office, I was shocked to see a crowd of some 300 people standing and watching me. I immediately thought, "We have an audience to preach the Gospel. This is great!" But I was quickly told that we had to leave immediately. There had just been a large riot between Hindus and Muslims and several dozen people had been killed. About 10 minutes later I realized we were in Raxaul, and I said to myself, "What a great place to set up a mission!" And so I did.

Winning a 5K in Algeria

I had the honor of traveling to Algeria with my friend, Steve to visit the displaced people group from the western Sahara, the Saharawi. Refugees have been living in exile for more than 50 years and in about four different camps. More than 250,000 of them live in the desert. Getting there was no easy task.

We flew from Spain to a small, private military airport in Algeria on a chartered flight. (There are not any flights directly to the refugee camps.) Some people in the international community were trying to raise awareness of their plight, so they were putting on a marathon through the desert. We went along, not as runners, but because my friend had been working among the refugees for several years in a desire to help.

A wide range of people came, not really caring about the Saharawi, but to run a marathon through the Sahara desert. One of the individuals who made it on our trip was Patch Adams, the guy from the movie portrayed by Robin Williams. A very unique man indeed. He did not run the marathon, but dressed up like a clown the entire time making children laugh.

They did have a 5k and 10k run, so I entered the 5k and the funny thing is, I think I won it. When I crossed the finish line, I was the first one to do so. However, at the reward ceremony they gave the prize to a local Saharawi. The humor in this is that I am not a big runner. I did not fight with the judges, realizing it would be good to empower the girl who they said won. It was a great journey and a reminder of the millions of people around the world who live in exile and as refugees.

Running into Some Houston Friends in Beijing

I was spending a few days in China after taking two pastors to India. The day before I was to leave, I was walking around a shopping market and looked up and thought I saw a man who looked like a youth pastor from Houston, Texas. To my amazement, it was. I shouted, "Jerome Smith!"

He looked at me with shock and said, "Joel Vestal?"

I said, "Yes!" He was from Tallowood Baptist Church, the very church that ordained me into ministry. He was in China with a group of students, ministering in orphanages. We shared dinner together that night, and it was a joy to hear the experiences of his High School and college students. It reminded me of the different experiences I had at that age and how many seeds were planted to be involved in global ministry. We said goodbye that night, but it was one of those moments God orchestrated so we could encourage each other.

A Thanksgiving Day I Will Never Forget

We approached a police road block at about 10 p.m. after driving for more than six hours from Kathmandu, Nepal. Albert and I had missed our flight coming from New Delhi, trying to get to ServLife India on the border of India and Nepal for our pastors' training conference. We had been in New Delhi for some meetings.

I realized our driver would not pass the road block, no matter much I tried to convince him to drive ahead. He said we would be shot with bullets from the RNA (Royal Nepal Army) if he drove past the road block, even though there was no one in sight on the road. We were surrounded by mountains and in the middle of nowhere. He said he did not want to die that night and neither did I; not because I fear death but because I want to grow old with my wife, watch my son grow up, have more children, and see the Gospel preached around the world.

So we turned around, realizing we were going to have to find a place to stay, but at this late hour it would be very difficult. We passed several houses all locked up and finally saw one small hut with a fire inside. We got out and were welcomed by a poor Nepali family along the road. We sat around their fire and shared stories. They said two days earlier 24 army soldiers had been killed on the road by Maoists and that was why the road blocks were there. They had also discovered 24 bombs that were being used to blow up supply trucks.

As the wife was telling us this, I saw a truck park right in front of her small house made of grass and mud. When the lady found out we had a children's home, she brought out a small girl and asked us to take her. She said her village of just 150 families had more than 45 orphans from the Maoists conflict. We told her our facility is not adequate to take more children, but would keep in touch with her. I wanted to tell her that we would take all 45, and perhaps one day we can.

We prayed for the family and shared the Gospel with her. We also gave her some extra medicine for the children in the community. She was happy. It was Thanksgiving Day when this happened, and I told her about the holiday. We were given an empty room in the hut and slept on a wooden floor with one blanket. It was very cold and I did not have proper clothing.

But as I laid down to sleep, cold and hungry, (I had only eaten one meal that day on our plane ride about 12 hours earlier), I began to ask myself, *Why am I here missing my son's second birthday? I am away from my wife, I'm cold and hungry. I could be many places right now with my family and here I am stranded in the middle of the mountains, surrounded by Maoist rebels, hiding out in a grass hut.* I realized at that moment it is the love of God that motivates me.

We woke at 5 a.m. the next day to drive to Raxaul, the home of ServLife India. After getting to the pastors' conference, I experienced a joy deep within my heart from seeing a dream become reality. God is about turning dreams into reality when they align with His redemptive purposes for a lost world. To see a movement of indigenous, young Indians giving their lives to preach the Gospel and start churches among their own people is what ServLife is all about. There is no greater cause in the world than seeing the love of God extend to every person on the globe.

The Hilton in Cairo and a Taxi in Jordan

I was in a Hilton Hotel in Cairo a few years ago trying to buy some postcards. You would think in a Five Star hotel all those working there would be more concerned about profit than principle; more concerned with the financial dealings of the day than faith. As I opened the door around 4 p.m., I accidentally hit a man with the door, not realizing he was standing that close. I tried to ask him, "Are you open?" No reply. I spoke the little Arabic I knew hoping he would reply to me. No reply. I looked down and saw a rug on the floor. He was facing toward Mecca and began to kneel down and pray—totally ignoring this guy who was only going to buy merchandise from his shop. No reply. No excuse. No sale.

On another occasion I hired a taxi to drive me from Aqaba to the capital, Amman. This is about a three-to four-hour drive through nothing but desert. After about two hours in the car with the winds gusting, the sand and the heat beating down on us, my Muslim driver stopped and asked if he could pray. I said yes, but did not think he would get out of the car. Sure enough, he got out and for 15 minutes prayed along the side of the road.

This is the sort of dedication to a life of prayer that I desire.

APPENDIX
B

Words of Wisdom from Around the World

"Wisdom makes one wise man more powerful than ten rulers in a city."—Ecclesiastes 7:19

These are words of wisdom I have heard from several places around the world. Many times I have found proverbs like these are good ways to start conversations with people from other lands. Just by asking what a particular proverb means, you demonstrate your interest in their culture and in them as individuals. Enjoy!

Africa

"Opinions founded on prejudice are always sustained with the greatest violence."—Hebrew language proverb of Israel, Southwest Asia

"If you damage the character of another, you damage your own."—Yoruba proverb of Nigeria, West Africa

"The bridge is repaired only after someone falls in the water."—Somali proverb of Somalia, East Africa

"Equality is not easy, but superiority is painful."—Serere proverb of Senegal, West Africa

"When your neighbor is wrong you point a finger, but when you are wrong you hide."—Ekonda proverb, Democratic Republic of the Congo (former Zaire), in Central Africa

"The tears running down your face do not blind you."— Togo, West Africa

"Without retaliation, evils would one day become extinct from the world."—Nigeria, West Africa

"If you have one finger pointing at somebody, you have three pointing toward yourself."—Nigeria, West Africa

"The one being carried does not realize how far away the town is."—Nigeria, Africa

"When the right hand washes the left hand and the left hand washes the right hand, both hands become clean."— Nigeria, West Africa

"Blessed are those who can please themselves."—Proverb from the Zulu nation (South Africa)

"When a fool is cursed, he thinks he is being praised."

"We start as fools and become wise through experience."

"The wind does not break a tree that bends."—Sukuma proverb of Tanzania, East Africa

"To engage in conflict, one does not bring a knife that cuts—but a needle that sews."—Zambia, East Africa.

"When a king has good counselors, his reign is peaceful."

"You can tell ripe corn by its look."

"Wood already touched by fire is not hard to set alight."

"Whom a serpent has bitten a lizard alarms."

"Whoever tells the truth is chased out of nine villages."

"Whether the knife falls on the melon or the melon on the knife, the melon suffers."

"When you live next to the cemetery, you cannot weep for everyone."

"When you know who his friend is, you know who he is."

"When there is no enemy within, the enemies outside cannot hurt you."

"When the blind lead the blind, both shall fall into the ditch."

"When the big tree falls, the goat eats its leaves."

"When elephants fight, it is the grass who suffers."

The Arab World

"In the desert of life the wise person travels by caravan, while the fool prefers to travel alone."

"A promise is a cloud; fulfillment is rain."

"After dinner, rest; after supper walk a mile."

"All sunshine makes the desert."

"An army of sheep led by a lion would defeat an army of lions led by a sheep."

"Dawn does not come twice to awaken a man."

"Death rides a fast camel."

"Dwell not upon your weariness, your strength shall be according to the measure of your desire."

"Example is better than precept."

"Examine what is said, not him who speaks."

"Go and wake up your cook."

"He who has health has hope; and he who has hope, has everything."

"On the first of March, the crows begin to search."

"The enemy of my enemy is my friend."

"The English are a nation of shopkeepers."

"It is good to know the truth, but it is better to speak of palm trees."

"On the day of victory no one is tired."

"Never speak ill of the dead."

"Never sit in the place of a man who can say to you, 'Rise.'"

"Live together like brothers and do business like strangers."

"Never give advice in a crowd."

"The whisper of a pretty girl can be heard further than the roar of a lion."

China

"A single kind word keeps one warm for three winters."

"Those who seek revenge must remember to dig two graves."

"A bad word whispered will echo a hundred miles."

"A bad worker quarrels with his tools."

"A bar of iron continually ground becomes a needle."

"A beautiful bird is the only kind we cage."

"A bird can roost but on one branch, a mouse can drink not more than its fill from a river."

"A bird does not sing because it has an answer. It sings because it has a song."

"A bit of fragrance always clings to the hand that gives you roses."

"A book holds a house of gold."

"A bride received into the home is like a horse that you have just bought; you break her in by constantly mounting her and continually beating her."

"A bridle for the tongue is a necessary piece of furniture."

"A chicken is hatched even from such a well-sealed thing as an egg."

"A child's life is like a piece of paper on which every passerby leaves a mark."

"A clever person turns great troubles into little ones and little ones into none at all."

"A client twixt his attorney and counselor is like a goose twixt two foxes."

"A cloth is not woven from a single thread."

"A closed mind is like a closed book; just a block of wood."

"A country where flowers are priced so as to make them a luxury has yet to learn the first principles of civilization."

"A courageous foe is better than a cowardly friend."

"A courtesy much entreated is half recompensed."

"A crisis is an opportunity riding the dangerous wind."

"A day of sorrow is longer than a month of joy."

"A dog in desperation will leap over a wall."

"A dog won"t forsake his master because of poverty; a son never deserts his mother because of her homely appearance."

"A fall into a ditch makes you wiser."

"A gem is not polished without rubbing, nor a man made perfect without trials."

"A good dog does not block the road."

"A good neighbor is a found treasure."

"A hasty man drinks his tea with a fork."

"A hasty man never wants for woe."

"A hundred men may make an encampment, but it takes a woman to make a home."

"A jade stone is useless before it is processed; a man is good for nothing until he is educated."
"A journey of a thousand miles begins with a single step."

"A man must make himself despicable before he is despised by others."

"A man must plough with such oxen as he has."

"A man need never revenge himself; the body of his enemy will be brought to his own door."

"A man's conversation is the mirror of his thoughts."

"A man's discontent is his worst evil."

"A nation's treasure: scholars."

"A person who says it cannot be done should not interrupt the man doing it."

"Don't cross the bridge until you come to it."

"Don't stand by the water and long for fish; go home and weave a net."

"Don't waste good iron for nails or good men for soldiers."

"Don't waste too many stones on one bird."

"Dream different dreams while on the same bed."

"Dream of a funeral and you hear of a marriage."

"Easier to bend the body than the will."

"Easier to rule a nation than a son."

India

"A person who misses a chance and the monkey who misses its branch can't be saved."

"When anger comes, wisdom goes."

"Agriculture is best, enterprise is acceptable, but avoid being on a fixed wage."

"Anger ends in cruelty."

"Blaming your faults on your nature does not change the nature of your faults."

"Don't just cross a river—cross it bearing fire!"

"Fate and self-help share equally in shaping our destiny."

"Garlic is as good as ten mothers."

"Keep five yards from a carriage, ten yards from a horse, and a hundred yards from an elephant; but the distance one should keep from a wicked man cannot be measured."

"Large desire is endless poverty."

"Life is not a continuum of pleasant choices, but of inevitable problems that call for strength, determination and hard work."

"Separation secures manifest friendship."

"The way to overcome the angry man is with gentleness, the evil man with goodness, the miser with generosity and the liar with truth."

"The weakest go to the wall."

"To the mediocre, mediocrity appears great."

"You can never enter the same river twice."

"You can often find in rivers what you cannot find in oceans."

"You can only lean against that which resists."

"Self praise is no praise."

"The young crow is wiser than its mother."

"What is play to one is death to another."

"In a treeless country, the castor-oil plant is a big tree."

"A scalded cat dreads cold water."

"The washerman never tears his father's clothes."

"A fool went to fish, but lost his fishing-basket."

"A thief is a thief, whether he steals a diamond or a cucumber."

"God takes care of a blind cow."

"One who cannot dance blames the floor."

Japan

"A frog in the well does not know the ocean."

"A wise person changes their mind."

"One can stand still in a flowing stream, but not in a world of men."

Tibet

"A father deserted by a wise son is like being caught in a shower without a felt."

"Excellent people are honored wherever they go."

"Goodness speaks in a whisper, evil shouts."

"The wise understand by themselves, fools follow the reports of others."

"The wish is father to the thought."

Miscellaneous

"Silence is better than speech."—Cambodia

"A handful of friends is better than a wagon full of gold."—Czech Republic

"Get to know new friends but don't forget the old ones."— Bulgaria

"You cannot buy a friend with money."—Russia

"Lions believe that everyone shares their state of mind."— Mexico

"To a good hearer, a good speaker."—Spain

"It does not require many words to speak the truth."— Native American

"Nice words are free, so choose ones to please another's ears."—Vietnam

ABOUT THE AUTHOR

Joel Vestal is a native of Texas but has lived all over the country. He did his undergraduate study at Baylor University and graduate work at Fuller Seminary in California. Joel has spoken for Leadership Network, *The Jesus Film* Project of Campus Crusade for Christ, the Baptist General Convention of Texas, David C. Cook Publishing (Future Gen Conferences), Soularize Conferences by the ooze.com, the Cooperative Baptist Fellowship, Wheaton College, Dallas Baptist University, Bethel College and many churches around the country. Joel sits on the board of WorldconneX, a missions ministry of the Baptist General Convention of Texas.

Joel and Elise are proud parents of Zayd Vestal, born November 27, 2002. They are also expecting their second child in August 2005. Currently, the Vestals make their home in Thailand. In 2004, they lived in four cities and three countries. They are hard to keep up with, but you can try by reading Joel's blog at: http://zaydsdad.typepad.com/

ABOUT SERVLIFE INTERNATIONAL, INC.

Joel Vestal started ServLife while a 19-year-old college student at Baylor University. As a result of walking through the streets of Calcutta, the hospitals of Baghdad, the villages of southeast Africa, the jungles of Indonesia, war torn Sudan, the slums of Cairo, the deserts of Algeria, and dictator-oppressed Cuba, it was obvious that an army of indigenous missionaries were eager to evangelize their own people but lacked the training, encouragement and support. Thus, ServLife was established.

ServLife exists to build global community by helping multiply the church and alleviate human suffering through working with indigenous/local Christian leaders. ServLife places an emphasis on taking the whole Gospel to the whole person.

Currently, ServLife has an international missionary staff of more than 50 people. ServLife works in about 12 nations and seeks to be a catalyst in seeing emerging generations and churches embrace the call of Jesus Christ to make disciples of all nations while championing the rights of the poor and oppressed. ServLife desires to enter and minister in areas of the world where the least amount of Christians are present and human suffering and injustice is the highest.

The areas that ServLife works in include:
- Church Planting and Evangelism
- Training of Indigenous Christian Leaders
- Orphanage Ministry
- HIV/AIDS Ministry
- Micro-Enterprise
- Empowering Women
- Stopping illegal human trafficking

ServLife is a post-denominational, evangelical missions organization and is governed by a board of directors. It does not receive funding from any particular denominational body in America but is solely supported by individuals, local churches, and foundations.

Please visit our web site at www.servlife.org to learn more about our efforts and explore ways you can get involved. Or write

ServLife International, Inc.
P.O. Box 79675
Houston, TX 77279

HOW TO ORDER THIS BOOK

There are several ways you can order additional copies of *Wanting More*:

1. Order online at www.7loaves.com (credit cards accepted)

2. Mail your request along with a check to:
    7loaves, Inc.
    P.O. Box 3610
    Ann Arbor, Michigan 48106-3610

3. Fax your order to: 734.769.7635 (Visa, MC, Amex, Discover, and Paypal accepted)

4. Email your order to:
    customerservice@7loaves.com

5. Order by phone by calling 7loaves, Inc., directly at 810.516.9571

Proceeds of the sale of *Wanting More* will go toward the mission work of ServLife International, Inc. Please know that you cannot order online for bulk orders.

ABOUT THE PUBLICATION OF

THIS BOOK

This is my first book. Several American publishers who talked with me expressed interest in publishing this book. Some people counseled me to get a publisher while others affirmed my decision to self-publish. I am sure this book would most likely be a bit different than what you are reading now if I had worked through a publisher. However, the main issue for me in deciding to self-publish this book was so I could see a higher percentage of the profits go to alleviating human suffering and engaging world evangelization, instead of supplementing the bank account of a multi-million dollar, profit-driven American publishing company.

I also hope that self-publishing this book will inspire other writers to self-publish. I realize some would not agree and would say that for marketing purposes an established publisher would help get the book out to more people and possibly produce more profits. But I am happy to see potentially more money go directly to serving the poor and to world evangelization.

ENDORSEMENTS FOR *WANTING MORE*

"Joel Vestal intertwines his unconventional life experiences with basic biblical principals. He has a heart for the world and cares more about meeting people's needs than following the 'American Dream.' Living a simple nomadic life, he has ministered to all types of people in 'out of the way' places. As much as possible, Joel prefers to work with and facilitate the ministry of nationals. He is sensitive to the leading of the Holy Spirit, aware of the power of prayer and seizes opportunities to share the Gospel. I recommend *Wanting More* to every mission-minded Christian and every mission-minded church."

Dr. Billy Kim
President, Baptist World Alliance
President, Far East Broadcasting Co.—Korea
Pastor Emeritus, Suwon Central Baptist Church
Seoul, Korea

"Joel Vestal has journeyed with the Lord of the harvest and has drawn upon his rich experiences to clearly present the message of the Gospel which will motivate any sensitive person for transformational action. *Wanting More* will indeed enrich the world wide community of Christ united by the love of the crucified."

Richard Howell, General Secretary
Evangelical Fellowship of India
New Delhi, India

"Most Christians are bored or ignorant about 'missions.' If you include yourself in one of those categories, then put on your seat belt and get ready for the ride of your life. Drawing on his own experiences in some of the remotest places in the world, in *Wanting More* Joel Vestal tells a vivid and compelling story that will both challenge and reenergize how you think about Jesus' commission to disciple the nations today. As crucial as proclamation and evangelism are, Joel argues that the goal of missions should be 'whole life transformational discipleship.' *Wanting More* ought to come with a warning label: this book may drastically change your outlook on a world in need of Christ's love. You may well decide to become a 'missionary' yourself!"

William W. Klein, Ph.D.
Professor of New Testament
Denver Seminary; Denver CO

"Joel Vestal has earned the right to speak. His perspective on the struggles and successes of the global emerging church will greatly broaden you. His call towards wholeness and incarnation among the poor will find eager ears. Mine included."

Andrew Jones, Consultant
Director of Boaz Project
Orkney Islands, UK
www.TallSkinnyKiwi.com

"Wanting More is an inviting, yet challenging expression of God's call to followers of Jesus to want more, to do more... to serve our fellow human beings. And by so doing, in the name of Christ Jesus, to be a faithful witness. Joel Vestal has trusted God to lead him in adventures for service around the world. God has given Joel exceptional insights and maturities far beyond his age. *Wanting More* is winsome and full of hope, declaring simply and from the heart how one can grow in God and service to man."

Bill Brian, Attorney & Partner
Courtney, Countiss, Brian, & Bailey, L.L.P
Amarillo, TX

"Joel Vestal is a living embodiment of Christ's command to take the Gospel to 'the ends of the earth,' and this book is a telling account of his remarkable journeys. From Sudanese refugee camps in Uganda, to the poorest slums of India, Vestal shares not only his rich ministry experiences, but also reveals the deep need for more Christians to leave their comfortable couches of [American] Christianity and join him in the fulfillment of the Great Commission. Simply put, Vestal is a man with a profound passion for spreading the message of God's love to the poorest regions of the world, and these captivating stories will leave you inspired to join him in that pursuit."

Craig Lewiston, PhD Student
Harvard-MIT Division of Health Sciences and Technology
Boston, MA

"As American Christians, much of our lives are spent running from pain. We literally hide in our churches, keeping the world's need, brokenness and tragedy at bay. That's why Vestal's book cuts so deep. Through riveting, incredible stories, he retrieves the plan of Jesus: run toward the pain—not away from it—and find God's light and life in its midst. A passionate, life-altering book."

Sally Morgenthaler
Consultant & Author of Worship Evangelism
www.sacramentis.com
Denver, CO

"After reading some of the stories of Joel's Kingdom adventures, I am reminded of another young passionate leader who was not afraid to go anywhere, do anything and take as many people with him. That man was William Borden, and his quote I think embodies God's call on Joel's life: 'No reserve, no retreat, no regret.' We all need Jesus' perspective for the Kingdom of God above all else. This book through its wonderful stories gives us insights into people we will never meet and places we will never travel, but who are close to the heart of God. Come experience the adventure..."

Daryl Heald, President
Generousgiving.org
Chattanooga, TN
www.generousgiving.org

"My wife and I know Joel Vestal. He is using his time, energies and capabilities to further God's Kingdom through ServLife International."

Mr. John Baugh, Founder & Senior Chairman
Sysco Corporation
Houston, TX

"*Wanting More* will entertain and challenge you with faith stories of adventure and daring that provide insight into the difference one person can make in seeking to achieve God's call to a holistic mission. Joel Vestal took a step of faith at an early age and has continued to see God work in ways that will challenge and inspire. If you are searching for how you can make a difference, you will find practical help and inspiration in Joel Vestal's vision for the Whole Gospel, the Whole Person, and the Whole World."

Samuel J. Voorhies, PhD
Director, Leadership & Organizational Development
World Vision International

"I have known Joel Vestal for a number of years. I have found him to be a man of God who has a heart to serve God and his people wherever they are. In this book, Joel has expressed the importance of a personal relationship with Jesus Christ and the compassion for people who do not know God. This book will challenge readers to grow in their spiritual life by the power of the Holy Spirit and to win lost people to Jesus Christ."

Rev. Dr. Simon Pandey, General Secretary & President
National Church Fellowship of Nepal (Member of World
Evangelical Fellowship)

"When Joel has something to say, I eagerly listen. Reading this book is like reading a thrilling mission adventure combined with theological challenge. *Wanting More* will not only help redefine mission for the church, but will help ignite your heart about what it means to be a follower of Jesus."

Dan Kimball, Author of The Emerging Church & Pastor of Vintage Faith Church Santa Cruz, CA

"Joel's writing combines an incarnational missiology with up-to-date global cultural awareness. His writing resonates with those seeking to connect those living in a pluralistic postmodern culture to the ongoing passion of God to draw people to himself from every tribe."

Ron Johnson, Lead Pastor Pathways Church Denver, CO

"I have known Joel for more than 10 years. I believe anyone who reads *Wanting More* will get insight into an aspect of what God is wanting to communicate to the church, especially in North America. This book is not just another missions book; it is the heart of what God is shifting us into for the harvest coming in our generation! You will definitely be encouraged and challenged by Joel's challenge to us."

Ty Denney, Associate Pastor & Director of Antioch Missionary Training School Antioch Community Church Waco, TX

"Joel Vestal writes from a depth of passion and experience few possess at his age. He touches our hearts, opens our ears to hear the cries of those who have never heard the Gospel, and gives us vision for the weeping of those who suffer neglect and abuse around the world. In these pages you will find the bright light of God's love in a new generation who are giving their lives for Christ among the poorest of the poor. As you travel with Joel Vestal to Africa, India and Indonesia, you will see the world with new eyes of compassion for the lost and neglected. Joel's passion for God and for the lost will disturb, inspire and challenge you."

Dr. Bill Tinsley, President
WorldConneX
Baptist General Convention of Texas
Dallas, TX

"Reading this book brings back the sparkle to the Great Commission—taking away various practices that have clung to it over the years. Joel invites us on a journey during which God renews in us the serious desire and commitment to serve God in accordance with the leading of the Holy Spirit. Who knows, God may lead you to His service as you read through the pages of this book. Do not hold back! I encourage you to accompany Joel Vestal on this wonderful journey."

Nabil Costa, Executive Director
Lebanese Baptist Society
Beirut, Lebanon

"In a cultural landscape of cheesy sitcoms and Reality TV, *Wanting More* is like a PBS documentary. Rich, poignant and powerful, Joel's passion for the Kingdom of God pulsates through every story."

Don Vanderslice, Pastor
Mosaic Church
Austin, TX

"For most of the history of the evangelical modern missions movement, we in the West have done the lion's share of the talking. Fortunately for us all, there is a new breed of missionary thinker and practitioner who has been gifted with the requisite humility to actually listen. Joel Vestal, along with the ServLife family, has demonstrated this ability, and, as such, is leading many of us to reconsider our background understandings of the Church's role in the world today. One of the global voices Joel is particularly attuned to is challenging the church in the West about its ability to imagine and enact a coherent social ethic that is simultaneously locally authentic and globally engaged. While various attempts are underway to renew evangelical thought and practice on this front, the vision I find most likely to make significant inroads in the years to come can be glimpsed amidst the pages of this book. My prayer is that you won't just read this book, but will instead allow God to read you through this book... then ask yourself a simple, yet life changing, question: How should I respond to what I am hearing?"

Richard Klopp, Pastor
Team Quebec Community
Quebec City, Canada

"Passion and experience collide in Joel's life and in this book. God is calling us to go and this book is part of your preparation to go now! *Wanting More* is dangerous reading for anyone who struggles with a selfish lifestyle."

Janice Henry, National Director
Teen Community Bible Study

"*Wanting More* layers story-beauty *with* meaning-hope. As the reader you are challenged and loved, silenced and encouraged to live out the biblical practices of prayer, compassion, justice and simplicity. As for the writer Joel Vestal, this title is his life, which makes *Wanting More* a must read for God's cause."

Greg Russinger, Lead Pastor
Bridge Communities, Ventura, CA
Co-designer of the Soliton Network & Sessions
www.solitonnetwork.org

"Outstanding! Joel Vestal is a young man who sees global missions work through the lens of experience, wisdom and Scripture. This book will keep the reader's interest while providing inspiration and instruction to pastors, missionaries and Kingdom workers who seek to obey the Great Commission."

Dave Divine, Lead Pastor
The Church at Chapel Hill (Assembly of God)
Douglasville, GA

"This book may cause your blood pressure to rise as you dream of the possibility of living fully in the will of God. It's an anecdotally-charged challenge to an arrogant American church, which is often more worried about changing homeland politics and building huge temples to their success than it is with living the Gospel out in the world so God's glory is evident and injustices are eradicated. Joel places the cookies on the bottom shelf and makes us realize that the mission God has called us to is more exciting than any "adventure" Reality TV can concoct."

Mike Gunn, Lead Pastor
Harambee Church
Seattle, WA

"A fresh perspective from an author who has lived what he is passionately advocating. Enter into his story as he abandons the 'American Dream' in pursuit of God's dream for the world. His reflections on cultures, religions and the poor will challenge and compel you to action. This is a cry to the western church to wake up and learn from our global neighbors what it means to be the body of Christ."

Shauna Rushing, Minister of Student Missions
The Woodlands United Methodist Church
The Woodlands, TX

"Joel has lived the whole gospel to the whole world better than most. That is why this book is not theory; it is authentic. Joel removes the walls that surround the western church and places us in the midst of the story of the whole church and lets us meet the real people who live out an amazing faith. This book is a must read because it critiques the Christianity of those of us in the West, and it fuels our hearts to want more than what we are experiencing. The new face of mission must be holistic and look more like Jesus, and Joel explains why. If you are wanting more from your faith and wanting to enlarge your view of Jesus' global community, then you have to read this book!"

> *Rick McKinley,*
> *Pastor of Imago Dei Community*
> *Author of Jesus in the Margins*
> *Portland, Oregon*

"Wow! You will need a passport after reading my friend, Joel Vestal's new book, *Wanting More*. He shakes us out of our slumber and reminds us we are citizens of two countries—here and heaven. This is a book for those who are more interested in building the Kingdom than building an earthly empire. And I would prescribe it for anyone suffering from 'been there, done that, now what?' syndrome. I built Student Leadership University on the philosophy that you and I will be the same five years from now except for the places we go, the people we meet, and the books we read. This is defiantly a life-changing book I'm recommending to our students."

> *Dr. Jay Strack, Founder & President*
> *Student Leadership University, Orlando, FL*
> *www.studentleadership.net*

"I have known Joel for several years and have visited an orphanage he founded in a part of Northern India widely known to be some of the hardest spiritual soil on earth. Joel is no 'arm chair missionary.' He speaks from a life filled with in-the-trenches experiences of God's Kingdom of justice and peace invading the most desperate situations imaginable. Read this book if you'd like to find out how you, too, can partner with God's mission. Joel is an able guide for us all."

Kevin Rains
Lead Pastor, Vineyard Central
Cincinatti, OH

"Joel Vestal is the Indiana Jones of the mission world. For years, he has traveled the world and has faced real life dangers to help spread faith, love and hope. Wherever he has gone, lives have been turned upside down— including mine. Joel's book will help you discover the dangerous life we have been called to live in order to share God's love—even in the darkest places. This book motivates and equips us to be a part of God's mission to the nations in a fresh and effective way."

Eric Bryant, Team Leader & Assistant Pastor
Mosaic Church
Los Angeles, CA

"INCREDIBLE! The book every Christian should read. Every page is anointed by the Holy Spirit. You cannot read this book without coming away with a passion for the souls of lost men and women."

Freddie Gage, Southern Baptist Evangelist
Euless, TX

"I felt energized by the passion that exuberated in my American friend Joel from the first time we met. I am encouraged to connect with the focused ministry of ServLife that's not only faithful to the heartbeat of Christ, but also in touch with the realities of where people are in various parts of the world. There's a strong respect for the local indigenous expressions of church and mission in these pages with snapshots of what genuine conversation, partnership and mutual learning look like. Joel takes us along his adventures and creates space for us to hear the call to follow Jesus here and now, starting where we are but also knowing we are participating in God's global purposes together."

Sivin Kit, Pastor
Bangsar Lutheran Church
Kuala Lumpur, Malaysia